Text, Role, and Context

THE CAMBRIDGE APPLIED LINGUISTICS SERIES

Series editors: Michael H. Long and Jack C. Richards

This series presents the findings of recent work in applied linguistics which are of direct relevance to language teaching and learning and of particular interest to applied linguists, researchers, language teachers, and teacher trainers.

In this series:

Text, Role, and Context

Developing Academic Literacies

Ann M. Johns

San Diego State University

CAMBRIDGE
UNIVERSITY PRESS

PUBLISHED BY THE PRESS SYNDICATE OF THE UNIVERSITY OF CAMBRIDGE
The Pitt Building, Trumpington Street, Cambridge CB2 1RP, United Kingdom

CAMBRIDGE UNIVERSITY PRESS
The Edinburgh Building, Cambridge CB2 2RU, United Kingdom
40 West 20th Street, New York, NY 10011-4211, USA
10 Stamford Road, Oakleigh, Melbourne 3166, Australia

First published 1997

Printed in the United States of America

Typeset in Sabon

Library of Congress Cataloging-in-Publication Data

Johns, Ann M.
Text, role, and context : developing academic
literacies / Ann M. Johns.
p.   cm. – (The Cambridge applied linguistics series)
Includes bibliographical references.
ISBN 0-521-56138-8. – ISBN 0-521-56761-0 (pbk.)
1. English language – Rhetoric – Study and teaching.   2. Academic
writing – Study and teaching.   3. Discourse analysis, Literary.
4. Reading (Higher education)   5. Literary form.
I. Title.   II. Series.
PE1404.J64   1997
808'.042'07 – dc20   96-43835
                                                          CIP

*A catalogue record for this book is available from
the British Library*

ISBN 0-521-56138-8 hardback
ISBN 0-521-56761-0 paperback

For Dad, who believed that we could do anything if we tried,

For Don, who made great things happen in the most unusual ways,

and

For David, whose encouragement, intelligence, humor, and love make my life a pleasure.

Contents

Series editors' preface

This newest book in the Cambridge Applied Linguistics Series is written by a scholar who, for many years, has been at the forefront of efforts to improve the understanding of the complex issues involved in preparing students for successful university studies. Ann Johns redefines the nature of English for Academic Purposes and offers a fresh perspective on a central aspect of this subject – the nature of what she terms *academic literacy*. The book presents a powerful theoretical framework for understanding the nature of academic discourse and a compelling argument for reexamining assumptions about how academic literacy can be taught.

Further, Johns shows that in order to understand what literacy is one must consider much more than an individual's ability to produce and understand written discourse. Understanding the nature of literacy involves knowing how knowledge is represented in different disciplines and contexts, being familiar with the strategies needed for understanding and organizing texts, knowing the social contexts in which texts are produced and read, being acquainted with the community and culture that produce and value certain texts and types of text, and knowing how previous experiences of literacy shape perceptions and expectations as to the nature of written discourse.

Johns argues that learners acquire literacy in particular social contexts, developing what might be termed *socioliterate competence* through exposure to the genres specific to those contexts. Writers and readers become part of communities, each with its own rules, norms, conventions, and cultures of literacy. She supports her beliefs by analyzing the assumptions underlying a variety of familiar and not-so-familiar genre types, both academic and nonacademic. Throughout, she provides a rich and complex picture of the nature of academic literacy and how it has been viewed from different theoretical, philosophical, and pedagogical perspectives, at the same time challenging many common misconceptions about academic literacy and how it can be taught.

She explores literacy from the perspective of students, language teachers, and regular faculty in academic institutions. The pedagogical approach that Johns recommends involves teachers and students collaboratively examining the interactions of texts, roles, and contexts.

Teachers of literacy are seen as mediators among students, faculty, and administrators; learners are encouraged to examine the nature of genres used within different academic and noninstitutional contexts. Johns demonstrates that there is much more to the teaching of academic literacy than mastering the conventions of style and register of a particular discipline. There is a need for literacy teachers to educate faculty in other disciplines as to the nature of academic literacy, for they often have a naive understanding of what is involved in an academic language program – and what can be achieved in such a program. Faculty in other disciplines need to realize that there is no single, unified literacy skill that can be taught once to students in any discipline, who will then become fluent writers in their subject areas.

One strategy Johns recommends is to engage subject specialists such as lecturers in law, business, or medicine in the analysis of the genre and literacy conventions of their disciplines. Nonlanguage-based faculty can thus come to recognize the assumptions within their own discourse communities concerning the nature of literacy. Johns describes a number of other strategies for involving literacy and content instructors in the collaborative exploration of the nature of literacy for their students, among them team teaching, interviews, and questionnaires. She describes how students of academic writing can be engaged in research into the nature of literacy in their disciplines – through text analysis, interviews, participant observation, journal writing, self-reflection, and exploration of the reading and writing processes they themselves employ.

This important book will therefore be of considerable interest not only to literacy practitioners but also to faculty in other disciplines, as well as to university administrators who want to better understand the nature and role of literacy within an academic community.

Michael H. Long
Jack C. Richards

Preface

What assists students to continue to develop as readers and writers? How can we prepare and motivate them to succeed not only in our literacy classes but in their academic and professional careers? How can we involve campus faculty and administrators in this essential literacy effort? Questions like these plague practitioners in academic institutions throughout the world, for we have taken on an enormous task: to educate and motivate students to confront a myriad of texts, roles, and contexts that we cannot possibly describe or predict with accuracy. The pressure on us is great: Our educational institutions expect us to succeed in an effort to prepare students for any rhetorical or linguist exigency that may arise, to "fix" student illiteracies once and for all so that they can get on with the "real" academic work.

In this volume I argue that the key words in our vocabulary should be "research," "motivation," and "preparation." In our classes we need to motivate students to be literacy researchers, open to and prepared for the many social and linguistic forces that may influence their literate lives. If our students are to succeed, however, we cannot work alone. Education to literate practices must be the responsibility of all instructors, whatever their disciplines. However, others on our campuses will not take up the cause unless they are invited. Therefore we must issue invitations that faculty, and administrators, cannot refuse. Literacy practitioners must act as mediators and consultants as we, and our students, work to make the advancement of literacies a campus goal.

This volume has been a long time in the making: My professional life and research have been devoted to the teaching of academic literacy for more than three decades. I began in 1961 as a young teacher of 13-year-olds in Flossmoor, Illinois. Then I followed my husband to East Africa, where I taught in a Kenya girls' secondary school just before that country's independence from colonial rule. When I returned to the United States, I moved on to secondary and community college teaching. Two years at the American University in Cairo (1970–1972) provided an opportunity to teach students from the Arab world while completing a degree in Teaching English as a Foreign Language (TEFL). When I returned again to the United States, I founded San Diego State University's

American Language Institute, an intensive program enrolling students from more than fifty countries. As soon as it became possible for Americans to teach in China, I spent a year as a Fulbrighter (1981–1982), working with literacy practitioners on the teaching of EFL reading and writing. After returning to the United States, I became a tenured faculty member in two university departments, Linguistics and Academic Skills (now Rhetoric and Writing Studies), where my literacy teaching and research, particularly with culturally diverse American students, has continued. In 1985, my colleagues and I used a grant from the California State University Chancellors' Office to establish the linked class program described in this volume. Since that time, I have continued to work overseas as well, leading short-term literacy and English for Specific Purposes seminars in Singapore, Italy, Spain, Algeria, Chile, Morocco, China, the former Yugoslavia, Cyprus, Pakistan, Russia, and Egypt.

Throughout my professional life, I have conducted research with my students and colleagues and immersed myself in the literature from a number of disciplinary and national perspectives. Recently, I have been greatly influenced by writings about the social construction of texts and theoretical discussions of "genre" and "discourse community." I use this reading, and my long experience as a teacher, in attempting to answer some fundamental questions about student literacies and practitioner roles and pedagogies.

In this volume I move back and forth from theory and research to practice. Chapter 1 includes a presentation of the recent history of literacy pedagogies, driven by theories about how literacy is acquired and maintained. Three theoretical camps and their pedagogical implications are discussed: the Traditional, the Learner-Based, and the Socioliterate. The chapter concludes with the argument that in approaching the reading and writing of texts within academic cultures, practitioners should draw from all three of these views, with the Socioliterate providing the central focus.

However, I do not argue for a single methodology in the traditional sense. Like Kumaravadivelu (1994), I acknowledge that we are in a postmethodological era, and thus to imply that there is *one way* to teach or learn complex literacies would be irresponsible. Suggestions are made for pedagogies and approaches to research and mediation; however, they can serve only as examples or starting points for practices that must be tailored for specific educational environments. Rather than a method, I would like to encourage an attitude of mind, one in which instructors and students, through research and practice, attempt to come to terms with the variety of factors influencing the processing and production of texts.

Chapter 2 focuses on a basic term in the social constructionist literature, *genre,* showing how this concept applies to the knowledge that readers and writers share. Chapter 3 continues this discussion, presenting some "homely" genres as well as some from professional, avocational, and academic contexts. Chapter 4 addresses the thorny issue of "discourse community," drawing from the literature that suggests a close relationship between communities of readers and writers and their genres. I note that many people identify with a variety of communities, groups that are often complex, stratified, and conflicted.

Chapter 5 begins a discussion of our unique roles as literacy practitioners, those that obligate us to operate outside our immediate reading and writing classrooms. I suggest that joint pedagogical and research endeavors with other faculty may be the most effective avenues for inviting our colleagues into the literacy enterprise. Chapter 6 focuses on our students, especially their research roles and their responsibilities to their own evolving literacies. I argue that, through text artifact collection and analysis, expert interviews, and observation, students can enrich their understandings of academic texts, roles, and contexts, and at the same time refine their approaches to text processing and production.

Chapter 7 identifies some core curricular design principles intended to enhance active learning and application of socioliterate practices. Chapter 8 includes some suggestions for putting these principles into practice in a variety of literacy contexts, using portfolios as the classroom management tool. In addition to providing some basic literacy models, I discuss the literacy program with which I have been involved for more than a decade, the Integrated Curriculum at my own university. Chapter 9 provides a brief review of the literature on communities of practice and a call for action.

It should already be evident that this volume extends beyond a discussion of literacy instruction to a vision of practitioners as mediators among students, faculty, and administrators. By taking this mediating role, we can collaborate with students in research, analysis, and preparation for future literacy texts, roles, and contexts. We can engender an attitude of mind that promotes evolving socioliterate theories and thoughtful approaches to the uncertainties that each new rhetorical context can bring. And while we do this, we need to invite discipline-specific faculty to become thoroughly involved in the literacy enterprise.

Thus the development of socioliterate practices should be viewed as a lifelong process, one which our reading and writing classes and our mediating efforts can promote but cannot hope to complete. Ultimately, our goals as literacy practitioners should be to cultivate a general interest and involvement in literacy on our campuses and to encourage among students approaches through which they can value and exploit their own languages and dialects, genres, and literacies while continuously adding to their literacy repertoires.

Ann M. Johns

Acknowledgments

I have been a teacher of literacy for more than 30 years and a student of literacy for more than 50. It would be difficult to thank all of those who have influenced me during my career, so I will have to focus on the people who have encouraged and assisted me in writing this manuscript during the past 5 years or so.

I asked a number of colleagues to read and comment upon drafts of various chapters. My thanks to Joan Carson, Liz Hamp-Lyons, Tom Huckin, Anne January, Heather Kay, Donna Price-Machado, Paul Prior, and Ellen Quandahl, whose comments assisted me in making major revisions. Many other colleagues, particularly English for Specific Purposes specialists in English as a Foreign Language contexts, have helped me to understand the application of the approaches described here to various educational environments. Ulla Connor's work on argumentation and coherence has influenced mine, and Tony Dudley-Evans has been both encouraging and informative. John Swales has been particularly supportive throughout my entire writing process: reading and commenting upon a number of draft chapters, sending me important articles, and urging me to "get on with it." I am grateful for his expertise, friendship, and encouragement.

I am also indebted to many faculty, students and administrators at my home university, San Diego State, in California. My colleagues in the former Academic Skills Center (now the Department of Rhetoric and Writing Studies) who design curricula and teach in the linked program, and the students who have been enrolled in this program over the years, have been my best instructors. The graduate students in my 1995 "Genre and Community" seminar gave me insights into the literature that helped me to think through the early chapters, as well as providing some useful research cited in this volume. Virginia Guleff and Carol Lowther, both graduate students and fellow teachers, have been splendid: reading various drafts, assisting me in organizing the references, and urging me on when I became ill and discouraged. Gladys Highly read, edited, and helped me to organize the chapters and my ideas throughout the writing of two drafts. Jackie Severance is responsible for the original illustrations, derived miraculously from my primitive hen scratchings. Janet Hamann assisted with the final review and completed the index.

Many discipline-specific faculty have taught in the linked class program described in this volume; however, Elizabeth Colwill (History), Jim Gerber (Economics), and Mary Kelly (Women's Studies) have made special contributions to my understanding of their disciplines and the nature of academic literacies. And I must not forget the administrators: Don Basile, who built and sustained our center through the best and worst of times; Leslie Johnson and Elise Miller, the talented Integrated Curriculum Program administrators; Carol Sweedler-Brown, our current chair; and the college deans, particularly Don Short (Sciences), Paul Strand (Arts and Letters), and Joyce Gattas (Professional Studies and Fine Arts), who have provided vital support for our campus efforts.

Cambridge University Press has been good to work with: Jack Richards was particularly encouraging when I was getting started, and Mary Carson, Mary Vaughn, and Olive Collen have been helpful at every juncture. The expert reviews have guided my several revisions, although I often wished for more agreement among reviewers.

My family has been wonderful throughout my entire academic career. Beth, Tim, and Mike seem to enjoy having a mother with crazy ideas who spends lots of time at the computer; David has listened for hours to my plans and worries and has educated me to his disciplinary practices.

I am indeed fortunate, personally and professionally; and this may be the reason why this volume is so optimistic about what can be accomplished. We literacy instructors have the most challenging and fascinating roles on our campuses and, for this reason, we need to involve everyone in our enterprise.

1 Literacy and pedagogy
Three views

It is within the students, of course, that the learning occurs, but it is within the teacher, who sits at the juncture of forces above, below and sideways that the learning situations are framed (Bazerman, 1994, p. 29).

If we write and teach [reading and] writing, we have a theory of [literacy] by definition (Zebroski, 1986, p. 57).

We all have theories: about politics, about art, about health, about relationships, about raising children – and about many other topics and events that are part of our everyday lives. Our theories, sometimes implicit and incomplete, help us to explain and to impose some order on the chaos of data that we experience. Most of us do not discuss our theories at an abstract level; in fact, we may not acknowledge that we have them. But we do. Sometimes we imply our theories through aphorisms. "Spare the rod and spoil the child" indicates a particular theory of childraising. "An apple a day keeps the doctor away" indicates a belief about the relationship between eating and good health.

There are fewer aphorisms about theories of literacy; instead, teachers tend to identify a commonly held theory and its pedagogical implications through a verbal shorthand: use of terms or phrases that other literacy practitioners are expected to understand. Teachers who subscribe to Traditional theories talk about "modes of writing" or "drill and practice." Those with Learner-Based theories speak of "the Writing Process" or "Whole Language." Teachers who espouse Socioliterate views talk about organizing their classroom through study of "genres."

But I am getting ahead of myself. First I need to discuss the term *literacy* itself, explaining why it has been chosen as the volume's guiding term; then I will turn to commonly held theories of literacy and pedagogy.

These questions will be addressed in the chapter:

1. How is literacy defined? Why is this term appropriate for this volume?
2. What basic theoretical elements must be considered in analyzing a theory of literacy and its pedagogical implications?
3. What are the elements that identify Traditional literacy theories? How

have these theories influenced pedagogies? What are the strengths and drawbacks of these theories?

4. What elements are central to the two major Learner-Centered theoretical camps, the Expressivist and the Psycholinguistic-Cognitive? What are some of the contributions to pedagogy made by those holding these views? What key terms have guided the Learner-Centered pedagogies? What problems can arise from the use of these theories and pedagogies, particularly with students who are culturally or linguistically diverse?

5. What is the focus of Socioliterate views? How can these views contribute to our pedagogies? In what ways do they draw from other theories and pedagogies? What problems can arise from our attempts to realize these theories in the classroom?

6. How can Socioliterate theories draw from other views to construct a rich pedagogical base?

Literacy defined

Let us begin, then, by defining a central term in this volume: *literacy.* Why has literacy been chosen from among the several terms that are available? First of all, it is much more inclusive than other terms that refer to some of the same phenomena. It is more inclusive than "reading and writing" because it requires an understanding that these "skills" are influenced by each other as well as by speaking and listening (Carson et al., 1992; Harris, 1990).[1] The term also encompasses ways of knowing particular content, languages, and practices. It refers to strategies for understanding, discussing, organizing, and producing texts. In addition, it relates to the social context in which a discourse is produced and the roles and communities of text readers and writers. This inclusive concept encompasses learning processes as well as products, form as well as content, readers' as well as writers' roles and purposes. Literacy is also employed to refer to a variety of previous experiences, not only with texts, but with parents, teachers, and others who are literate (Gee, 1991; Heath, 1986). What this term does is integrate into one concept the many and varied social, historical, and cognitive influences on readers and writers as they attempt to process and produce texts. Admittedly, it is a complex and problematic term, but becoming literate, particularly in academic contexts, is even more complex and problematic, an argument that will be made throughout this volume.

---

1 In some English as a Foreign Language (EFL) contexts, only one English literacy "skill," reading, is taught and learned. In these contexts, academic literacy can and should refer to reading only.

If we are to discuss becoming literate, then the term must be pluralized ("literacies"), for there are many literacies, especially in academic settings, acquired in different ways and for different purposes. For a variety of reasons, some of us can read literature more effectively than we can read engineering texts, generally because of our past experiences, personal motivations, or community affiliations. As professionals, we can write successfully for some academic journals, yet our manuscripts are rejected by others. Therefore, at any time, a literate person relates in a more sophisticated manner to some texts, roles, and contexts than to others. And individual literacies change. Their evolution is influenced by a person's interests, cultures, languages, and experiences, and by responses of others to their texts. It is important to note that literacy growth is not incremental; instead, it involves "ongoing processes of perpetual transformation, dynamic and synthetic" (Neilson, 1989, p. 5).

We practitioners, and our students, come to classes with theories about what it means to be literate and about how literacy is acquired – theories that are often unacknowledged or explored. Despite the hidden and sometimes incomplete nature of these theories, they influence how academic literacies are taught and learned. Therefore it is important for us to explore our literacy theories and their origins and, if appropriate, to revise and expand them in order to promote a repertoire of literate practices among our students.

In sum, literacy has been chosen as the central term for this volume because it reflects the complexity and evolving nature of literacy acquisition and the influence of literacy theories on classroom practices. The term is used to remind us that we have much to consider: our own theories of academic literacy acquisition and those of our students; the ways in which our theories take pedagogical shape; and how we can encourage students to continue their literacy growth throughout their lives.

Basic theoretical elements

In this section I discuss the elements of a literacy theory, a theory in which acquisition, theories of text and language, and classroom practices are integrated.[2] I have chosen to integrate literacy theory with pedagogy because I believe that for most practitioners, application of theory takes place every day in our classrooms, whether we are aware of it or not.

---

2 At this point I am not distinguishing between first (L1) and second language (L2) literacy because, for the most part, the same theories have been applied in both L1 and L2 contexts.

The nature of acquisition

What basic, interrelated elements are essential to describing a literacy theory and its immediate pedagogical implications? One factor is the nature of acquisition: A theory of literacy must include beliefs about how abilities to read and write are acquired. Acquisition theories vary considerably among practitioners. There are those who believe that only after long, systematic exposure to oral language can literate behaviors be developed. This was one of the basic tenets of the Audiolingual Method, which is closely related to the Traditional views discussed in this chapter (see Richards & Rogers, 1986, pp. 44–63). Whole Language advocates, on the other hand, generally believe that only through using all four "skills" (speaking, listening, reading, and writing) simultaneously and experimenting with language can students acquire literate behaviors (see Heald-Taylor, 1991). Others believe that literacy is so closely tied to social forces that learners should consciously relate texts to culture in each of their literacy experiences (see Chapman, 1994; Cope & Kalantzis, 1993). All these beliefs about literacy acquisition have direct and immediate implications for the classroom.

The learner's role in the acquisition process

A related theoretical element is the nature of the learner and the role the learner plays in literacy acquisition. Is the learner a passive recipient of data as adults model the language? Must the learner drill and practice the correct forms in order for literacy to be acquired? Traditional theorists tended to view the learner in this way. Or is the learner an active participant in the process, the prime motivator and meaning-maker, as many Learner-Centered practitioners tend to believe? Is the learner caught between his or her own motivations and purposes and the constraints of the context and culture, assumptions made by some Socioliterate practitioners? Theories about the roles of learners in literacy acquisition are basic to our pedagogical choices.

The teacher-expert's role

A third important element in a literacy theory is a view of the role of the literacy teacher, or any adult expert, in the literacy acquisition process. Is this person the role model, the source of knowledge, and the director of learning, as is the case in many Traditional approaches? Is he or she the facilitator in the process of exploring and producing texts, as is often true in Learner-Centered classrooms? Or is the expert an intermediary, the arbitrator between the learners and the worlds of language and literacy into which they wish to be initiated, as suggested by some practitioners espousing Socioliterate views?

The nature of language and texts

A fourth element in literacy theory and pedagogy relates to the nature of language and of texts: their basic and fundamental features and their place in the world.[3] Are languages and texts principally formal, primarily grammatical patterns and rhetorical structures, as was suggested by many Traditionalists? Or are texts produced creatively by individuals, whose search for meaning supersedes form and other text features, as was suggested by the Expressivists holding Learner-Centered views? Conversely, are languages and texts socially constructed, produced through the intersection, tensions, and negotiations between individual purposes and the constraints of contexts, as argued by the social constructionists?

When we contemplate literacy theories and the pedagogies that stem from them, we need to think about each of the elements mentioned here: how literacy is acquired, the role of the learner in the acquisition process, the role of the expert in encouraging acquisition, and the nature of language and texts. Of course, each of these elements is influenced by the others. Our view of acquisition, for example, determines our view of the learner, and so on. In the sections that follow, three popular literacy models will be discussed. Each addresses the basic theoretical elements – but in different ways. Perhaps the most important to understanding the differences between these models is to identify the core element: the particular issue that drives the rest of the theory and resultant pedagogy. In the Traditional views, the core is the formal properties of texts, their macrostructure and grammar. In the Learner-Based views, it is the students' meaning-making processes that drive the other elements of the theory. The Socioliterate theorists begin with the community and culture in which texts are read and written and the social influences of the context on discourses. Though many of our pedagogies are a mix of these theories, we, and our textbooks, tend to favor one of the core elements. If we tape our own classroom activities or if we interview our students, we will probably find that we lean toward one theoretical camp more than the others.

---

3 In her very useful volume on contrastive rhetoric, Ulla Connor (1996, pp. 19–21) makes careful distinctions between texts ("discourse without context") and discourse ("text plus context"). Here, I use text and discourse interchangeably, referring always to what is written.

Traditional views and pedagogies

The first view to be discussed, often called Traditional, traces its origins to the European Enlightenment and the founding of modern science. Cope and Kalantzis (1993) argue that one of the reasons for the persistence of Traditional views is that they are based on a "scientific positivism" that originated in eighteenth-century Europe and North America and persists to this day. Applied to language, the Traditional view is seen in this way:

> [T]he [linguistic] world can be described in terms of "facts," rules and regularities epitomized in tables to conjugate verbs or decline nouns. Language, it seems, is something that can be meaningfully visualized into tables arranged across the two-dimensional space of the textbook page (Cope & Kalantzis, 1993, p. 3).

This scientific, positivistic, "factual" view of literacy became the motivating force in the 1960s and 1970s, when applied linguistics research was devoted primarily to feature counts, the listing of particular grammatical or semantic features within certain types of texts (see Bhatia, 1993, pp. 5–6). There is a long and rich history of feature counts in applied linguistics, one that has strongly influenced teaching, particularly in English for Specific Purposes programs (Swales, 1988a). Researchers have found, for example, that in scientific and technical texts, there are concentrations of the passive voice and noun compounds; in literary essays, there is dependence on descriptive adjectives. These counts, made through scientific analysis and now conducted by computer, continue to be the basis for many Traditional teaching and assessment programs.[4] In these programs, students of science study those grammatical features that researchers have found to be common in science texts. The curricula for students of business are based on identified features of business discourses, and so on. Unfortunately, teachers and students in Traditional classrooms generally do not ask why these feature concentrations appear in particular texts, or what personal or social factors influence linguistic choices. Instead, they devote their time to studying lists of grammatical and lexical "facts" as they have been discovered through quantitative research.

Stemming from this factual, positivistic orientation is the insistence on the production of perfect texts and a single interpretation of a reading or vocabulary word. In many Traditional literacy classrooms, the focus continues to be on the teacher-directed study of grammar and vocabulary and the student production of perfect English sentences and discourses. Many

---

4 Of course, computers have also been excellent tools for other data analyses that have influenced pedagogies. See, for example, Francis (1994) on the uses of natural language corpora for the classroom.

teachers believe that until their students understand and can produce perfectly a sentence and its components, they cannot go on to reading or writing longer discourses such as the paragraph or essay. In these classrooms, student writers drill orally, copy, and memorize correct grammatical forms so that they can write error-free sentences and eventually produce perfectly structured, error-free texts.

In North America, composition theory extended these factual, scientific views of literacy into what have been called Current-Traditional approaches to writing. In these approaches, which continue to influence many modern literacy textbooks and classrooms, the emphasis is on formal, "factual" text organization. Written texts are categorized into "rhetorical modes," identified ways of organizing content at the paragraph or discourse level. Mode categories include "illustration, exemplification, comparison, contrast, partition, classification, definition, causal analysis, and so on" (Silva, 1990, pp. 14–15). Students are asked to practice these modes by imitating their forms, much as students in grammar-based classes practice correct forms at the sentence level.

Though the pedagogies based on feature counts and Current-Traditional approaches are somewhat different, they both have the same basic interest: surface-level, formal descriptions of what are considered to be standard language or discourse patterns, the "facts" of language.[5] Often these factual descriptions are broken down into a series of lists: of verbs and their morphologies, of noun phrases, or of types of discourse modes. The belief is in the purity and primacy of form and in the value of the quantitative studies of language features. Language is form(al); all other linguistic, psychological, and social factors are secondary, or in some cases, ignored.

The core elements of Traditional theories have been implied, but they will be summarized here. Literacy is acquired through directed practice, focused on the production of perfect, formally organized language patterns and discourses. Good learning is good habit formation, and "good habits are formed by giving a correct response rather than making mistakes" (Richards & Rogers, 1986, p. 50; see also Skinner, 1957). The learner is a passive recipient of expert knowledge and direction. Not surprisingly, the role of the teacher is that of expert and authority, the person who directs all student learning. And what of the language and text? For Traditional literacy theories, language and textual *forms* are central. Good textual habits are acquired through practicing – even copying – correct texts. Classroom exercises expose students to discourse modes (definition, illustration) or direct practice of grammatical pat-

---

5 Current-Traditionalists are much less concerned with disciplinary concentrations of features. They believe that the textual modes that they teach can be found in any discipline.

terns. The Traditional literacy theories thus begin, and often end, with form: the formal syntactic patterns of the language and the formal organizational patterns of written texts.

Despite this critical commentary, it is important to acknowledge that Traditional approaches still provide food for thought, particularly for teachers of students for whom English is a second or foreign language. As practitioners, we certainly need to address issues of linguistic and textual form in our classrooms,[6] and we need to help our students to produce correctly edited texts. Unfortunately, however, many Traditional teachers and textbooks stop there, concentrating exclusively on drill, correction, and form to the detriment of all other considerations. Sentences are seen as mere formal patterns, and texts are portrayed to students as empty jars, with predefined configurations into which content is poured. Students are asked to "Write a comparison/contrast paragraph" or to produce sentence patterns, without consideration for the functions that these structures serve, writer or reader roles, context, topics, or the many other factors that influence the nature of text processing and production. Thus, though Traditional theories and pedagogies can assist us and our students to understand the importance of form and classroom practice, they are insufficiently rich to provide a complete understanding of what it means to be literate or to teach literacies for academic contexts.

Learner-Centered views and pedagogies

In the history of literacy theories, as in other theoretical areas, there have been major paradigm shifts (Kuhn, 1970). During these shifts, a theoretical view that has been central to pedagogies is challenged in the literature by another theory with a considerably different focus. Since the early 1970s, the reaction against Traditionalism has been strong and continuous. One important criticism of Traditional theories is that individual readers and writers, their meanings, their motivations, and their "voices," have been ignored. Because of this, the focus of many classrooms has shifted from concentrating on grammar facts and discourse modes to the motivations of individual readers and writers, to Learner-Centered stances. Inspired by Progressivists such as Dewey (1916), and more recently by postmodern theories of education such as those proposed by Aronowitz and Giroux (1991), Learner-Centered teachers argue that schooling can be successful only if it is directly relevant to students and their lives. Literacy is thus acquired as students seek meaning and process texts that are of interest to them. Not surprisingly, the students

---

6 See the excellent article by Richard Coe entitled "An apology for form; or, who took the form out of the process?" (1987).

are central to these theories and pedagogies. In many Learner-Centered classes, the teacher "is no more than a facilitator who gives students space to voice their own interests in their own discourses" (Cope & Kalantzis, 1993, p. 5). What about the role of texts and grammar? In many Learner-Centered theories, there is no recognized, standard set of language forms that is superior to others, no fixed facts of language that are scientifically determined and appropriate for all occasions. Instead, there are acceptable variations in language, form, and topic, many of which are brought to the classroom by linguistically and culturally diverse students. Thus, literacy is primarily about individual meaning-making, not about form. Meaning is made by students as they write discourses on topics of their own choosing or as they interpret readings in their own, individual ways. Teachers are not authorities or fact dispensers, as they are in many Traditional classrooms. Instead, they are coaches, facilitators who assist students in finding their own meanings and in developing cooperative and supportive classroom communities.

In the sections that follow, two somewhat different Learner-Centered literacy views will be presented: the Personal-Expressivist and the Psycholinguistic-Cognitive, both of which have contributed to major changes in literacy classrooms.

Personal-Expressivist views

Concern for the student as a unique individual with a "tale" to tell (Elbow, 1981), as one who must feel empowered to produce or deconstruct texts in individual and creative ways, is one important Learner-Based stance. Proponents argue that without this active personal involvement and a sense of control over texts, lifelong literacy growth is not worthwhile – or even possible.

The most vocal of the personal literacy advocates have been the Expressivists. For this group, writing is considered "an art, a creative act . . . the self discovered and expressed" (Berlin, 1988, p. 484). In a class based on Expressivist theory, the emphasis is on self-discovery and development of a unique, personal voice. Writing and reading journals that resemble personal diaries are encouraged. Students jot down their thoughts and experiences in these journals, reviewing them when preparing to write. The journals are the students' own personal records, and though the instructor may respond to their content, they are not corrected for errors (Peyton, 1987). In Expressivist classes, students may also write poetry or other discourses that help them in expressing their ideas and developing their creativity. Throughout, the focus is on a personal voice and individual interpretation in reading and writing.

Several approaches to literacy draw from Expressivism. Whole Language, an international movement in the primary and secondary schools, views "writing as a means of discovering for oneself what one thinks" (Rigg, 1991, p. 522). Whole Language reading, principally of literature, also involves personal meaning-making, because individual, and varied, interpretations of texts are encouraged (Edelsky et al., 1991). In Whole Language, and in other approaches that draw from Expressivism, the effort is made to liberate students from outside constraints so that they can write and read freely and creatively.

As practitioners, we can certainly learn from Expressivist theory and pedagogies. Consideration of individual students and their purposes for developing literate practices is essential to successful teaching and learning. Journals can establish fluent and frequent writing habits, and encouraging student selection and interpretation of texts can be highly motivational. However, focusing exclusively on personal literacy and creativity can be detrimental to the development of students as readers and writers within academic contexts. As many of our students already know, they cannot be "free" because, as they read and write, they are consistently influenced by their teachers and by examinations, their home cultures, their values and languages, and the contexts in which they are writing. At some point, students must contend with issues of grammar and form and with public contexts for writing. Expressivism often does not prepare them for these literacy experiences (see Raimes, 1991).

The freedom to write creatively about any topic is closely related to the development of "personal voice." Ramanathan and Kaplan (1996), however, argue that "voice" is a Amerocentric concept, which is highly problematic for students who are not mainstream North Americans because these students are not accustomed to speaking or writing in social contexts with "personal voices." Muchiri et al. (1995) support this argument, pointing out that many cultures "value a voice that identifies one with a group and doesn't make one stand out" (p. 181). In Tanzania, for example, students "tend to take on various collective personae, associated with traditional speech events" (p. 181) when they write. They may write in the voices of great authorities (such as famous authors), the government, or a village or family leader. Undoubtedly, students from other cultures in which group identification is strong, such as Japan, China, and Vietnam, may also find the concept of "personal voice" quite foreign and difficult, not to mention inappropriate to many social contexts.

Therefore, while we may draw from Expressivist views in helping students to develop fluency, confidence, and their personal literacies, we must also consider, at the very least, issues of form and social context. The most important academic discourses are public, requiring the consideration of textual constraints, the roles of readers and writers, and the context.

Psycholinguistic-Cognitive views

Another, considerably different, Learner-Centered cluster of views falls under the Psycholinguistic-Cognitive (PC) rubric. Rather than concentrating solely on personal expression, these theories have individual cognitive development and text processing at their core. PC views have revolutionized the teaching of literacy over the past 20 years or so, moving many pedagogies from a Traditionalist study of isolated text forms to classrooms that provide a "collaborative workshop environment within which students, with ample time and minimal interference, can work through their composing processes" (Silva, 1990, p. 15).[7] In the necessarily reduced discussion that follows, I present five key terms in the PC literature, each of which has contributed to the purposes and discussions of this volume: schemata and interactivity, text processing, strategies, and metacognitive awareness.[8]

SCHEMATA AND INTERACTIVITY

In the late 1970s and early 1980s, a literacy term employed by many PC theorists, particularly in reading, was *schema* (pl. *schemata*), referring to the prior knowledge that individuals bring to current reading and writing situations. Schema theorists argue that when readers or writers confront situations in which they need to process texts, they draw from their schemata, their past experiences with text content and form, to assist them in their processing. For example, if a reader begins a story about houses, she will draw from her past content experiences to conceptualize "house" and from her experiences with form to process the narrative structure of the text. However, if either the content or the form are foreign to this reader, she may have difficulty processing and comprehending the discourse. In schema-theoretical views, then, there is an interactive dialogue between text writer and reader, successful if they share schemata. In many cases, particularly in ESL and EFL classrooms, schemata are not shared by student readers and expert native-speaker writers; thus literacy instructors prepare students for the academic texts they will read (or write) by providing schema-development exercises. We often see prereading exercises in textbooks, such as semantic mapping, that develop and interrelate text vocabulary (see Feathers, 1993). In semantic mapping, students are given a key word, such as "balloon," from the title of the reading. Then they brainstorm about other words that might be related to the key word, constructing a "map" in which "balloon" is at the center. Textbooks may also have prereading questions to

7 See also Johns (1990a).
8 For an overview of Psycholinguistic-Cognitive reading issues, see Barnett (1989); for writing issues, see Leki (1992).

assist students in schema development. These questions, often relating to content, might be something like the following: "Have you ever seen a balloon?" "What do we know about balloons?" Schema theory has influenced writing as well; many textbooks ensure that students read about a topic and practice topic vocabulary before they begin to write. Expanded views of schemata and interactivity will appear when Socioliteracy is discussed at the end of the chapter.

TEXT PROCESSING

Mention of schema theory (prior knowledge) and interactivity between readers and writers leads directly to the central focus of Psycholinguistic-Cognitive literacy theories and pedagogies: individual text processing. Text processing is the core and driving element of the several pedagogies based on Psycholinguistic-Cognitive views. What has come to be called the Process Approach has been central to many journal articles over the past decade or so and has inspired numerous literacy volumes for teachers and students. These volumes tend to advocate the teaching of reading and writing processes together, encouraging their constant interaction. One reason for promoting this combining of "skills" is that reading and writing processes are considered to be "similar acts of construction and response" (Tierney, 1985, p. 110), requiring planning (prewriting or prereading), drafting (initial writing or reading), revising (modifying and extending), and editing (correcting or rereading).

What is the role of the teacher in this pedagogy? In a Process writing classroom, as in an Expressivist one, the teacher coaches, but does not direct, the students:

[The] teacher's role is to help students develop viable strategies for getting started (finding topics, generating ideas and information, focusing, and planning structure and procedure), for drafting (encouraging multiple drafts or readings), for revising (adding, deleting, modifying, and rearranging ideas); and for editing (attending to vocabulary, sentence structure, grammar, and mechanics) (Silva, 1990, p. 15).

Cooperation among students is also encouraged. Integral to most PC literacy classrooms is workshopping in groups and peer editing of student drafts. Although there are several models for these practices, the general view is that as students develop their own texts and processes, they need to read and evaluate other students' texts as well. In the classroom, students work actively in pairs or groups with each other's texts while the teacher moves about to keep them on task and answer questions. PC advocates are proud of the fact that their classrooms are not "teacher-fronted"; instead, the students work cooperatively to achieve their ends, calling on the teacher for assistance when it is needed.

The importance of Psycholinguistic-Cognitive theory and the Process Movement to the teaching of academic reading and writing cannot be overstated. Many classrooms have moved away from focusing on "perfect" sentences and texts as established by an "objective, scientific standard" (as in Traditional approaches) to viewing reading and writing as individual, varied, and process-based. In PC classrooms, students are encouraged to work in stages: to plan, to revise, to rethink, and finally, to edit. During this process, they workshop or peer-review their texts with other students, often becoming better critics of their own advancing literacies. Teachers generally tell students to discover their own meanings and purposes – uninhibited, initially, by issues of form, role, or context (Zamel, 1984), for, especially in writing, "form grows organically to fit the subject matter" (Coe, 1987, p. 16).

STRATEGIES AND METACOGNITIVE AWARENESS

With these text processing discussions come concerns for readers' and writers' strategies for completing tasks, "the management of interactions with the written text" (Carrell et al., 1989, p. 648). Possible strategies for processing readings or completing writing assignments are many. In reading, students may memorize, reread, take notes, or summarize (see Feathers, 1993, pp. 53–83). In writing, students may outline or draw a visual representation of their texts, ask others to comment, read their texts aloud before revision, or rely on dictionaries or thesauruses for new vocabulary (Leki, 1992, pp. 76–87). Analyzing and discussing individual strategies for text processing are important activities in many PC classrooms. In this effort, teachers encourage students to develop a metacognitive awareness of their processes, an ability to think about the particular strategies they use to complete a task. How students go about reading or writing a text (their strategies) and their metacognitive awareness of these efforts are essential to many PC views.

Learner-Centered views are rich resources for pedagogy. Theorists and practitioners holding these views believe that literacies are acquired through individual motivation and meaning-making or through processing and revising texts. The students are central to the acquisition process as they make choices, develop and comprehend their chosen texts, and analyze their strategies for text processing. Teachers are coaches and facilitators who interfere only minimally in a learner's reading and writing processes.

The Learner-Centered approaches have radically changed literacy theory, research, and practice in a variety of pedagogical contexts, from a focus on linguistic and textual form to a focus on individuals whose meaning-making and individual text processing are central. However, Learner-Centered views may not provide adequately for all students, particularly those who are culturally, socially, or linguistically distant from English academic languages and discourses. The pedagogical approaches often do not provide the necessary support and introduction to the language, tasks, and texts in academic or professional contexts with which students have had little or no experience. In fact, the kind of "insidious benevolence" in Learner-Centered classrooms that encourages student meaning-making and pays little attention to the social construction of texts may "promote a situation in which only the brightest, middle-class monolingual students will benefit" (Martin, 1985, p. 61). The very students we are attempting to encourage are left out.

Throughout this volume, I will draw from the rich contributions of the Traditional and Learner-Centered theories; however, I will argue that neither can provide an adequate basis for an instructional program that addresses academic literacies. Instead, I will argue for a view that texts are primarily socially constructed and that we should make this argument the center of our classroom practices. The next section will begin the discussion of Socioliterate views that will continue throughout the volume.

Socioliterate views and pedagogies

In many parts of the world, the literacy theory paradigm is already shifting, as practitioners come to terms with the limitations of Learner-Centered and Traditional pedagogies, particularly for diverse students in academic and professional contexts. One reason for this shift is the realization that individuals cannot, and often do not wish to be, completely "free" to make meaning and create "new" texts. Our students are aware of the social construction of discourses; they know that they are influenced, and judged, by the cultures and languages from which they come and into which they hope to enter.

For these reasons, I will return again to theory, to consider views that have at their core the social factors in literacy development. Here, I refer to these views as "Socioliterate," but they are closely related to what others call Social-Constructionist (Cook-Gumperz, 1986) and Socio-Cognitive (Geisler, 1991). In Socioliterate views, literacies are acquired principally through exposure to discourses from a variety of social contexts. Through this exposure, individuals gradually develop theories of genre (see Chapter 2). Those who can successfully produce and process texts within certain genres are members of communities, for "[academic] learning does not take place independent of [these] communities" (Brown & Duguid, 1995, p. 10). Learners are thus viewed as "social beings, achieving a sense of identity through learning to enter with increasing confidence into the ways of working" that are features of particular communities or cultures[9] (Christie, 1993, p. 100). Socioliterate views are

9 In Australia, where Socioliterate theories are well accepted, "community" is broadly defined in terms of a general culture. In the United States, "community" is more narrowly defined, as will be seen in Chapter 4.

translated into classroom practice in a number of ways throughout the world. This volume presents my particular translation, based on reading widely in the literature and many years of experience. In this view, the role of learners is an active one: Students are constantly involved in research into texts, roles, and contexts and into the strategies that they employ in completing literacy tasks within specific situations. Teachers provide leadership, for they introduce texts from various genres to students, and they act as mediators within academic contexts (see Chapter 5).

The text and language elements of the Socioliterate approach described in this volume draw extensively from the work of M. A. K Halliday,[10] who speaks of language as a "social semiotic," a resource employed to transmit and reformulate essential patterns of culture (1978) as realized in the valued texts of members of that culture. For Halliday and others (see Christie, 1993; Kress, 1985; Martin, 1985), language (and genres[11]) are integral to a social context. There is no artificial separation between what is in a text, the roles of readers and writers, and the context in which the text is produced or processed. Genres are thus the central elements of the theory, yet texts from a genre are always seen as "vehicles for communication" (Johns & Davies, 1983) within a culture, rather than "tales" that individuals tell (Elbow, 1981) or autonomous objects for study. Genres provide ways for getting things done among readers and writers whose cultures and communities mold their literacy practices.

Schemata and interactivity redefined

In this Socioliterate theory, what happens to the interpretation of schemata and interactivity, two central literacy terms? In the section on Psycholinguistic-Cognitive views of literacy, I noted that PC theorists generally define schema(ta) as the prior knowledge of text content and form that readers and writers bring to text processing. Students are most often prepared to read or write through enrichment of their understanding of topics and vocabulary, and, in rare cases, text structures.[12] However, there is much more than text content and form in a literate person's genre schemata. Considerable knowledge about context, about readers' and writers' roles, and about the values and registers of cultures and communities also affect genre knowledge. Developing these contextual, sociocultural schemata can be the key to successful processing or produc-

10 The volume is also very much influenced by Berkenkotter and Huckin (1995) and Swales (1990).
11 *Genre* will be defined and discussed at length in Chapters 2 and 3.
12 Because form is played down in PC views, it is often ignored in classroom schema-based activities (see Coe, 1987).

tion of a text that is appropriate to a particular situation. This is why Purves (1991, p. 62) argues that:

A great part of becoming literate is learning not only the textual conventions but also the conventional acts of a particular community and thus becoming a part of that community as it engages in the activity of literacy. Recent cognitive psychology has tended to support this view, suggesting that literacy involves the acquisition of knowledge that is arranged as schemata, or as chunks. Such knowledge includes semantic knowledge, or content, as well as linguistic or rhetorical structure. . . . [However,] this view is too limited . . . schemata should be broadened to include models of the structure and style of various types of discourse in certain situations . . . it should also include the functions of certain texts within a culture.

Therefore, the Socioliterate view proposed here expands the concept of schemata to include not only the readers' and writers' prior knowledge of text content and form but of the situations and the communities for which texts from a genre serve identified purposes. A theory must include the texts themselves, but also the roles of readers and writers and the communities for and in which texts are written. Central to reading and writing as viewed in a Socioliterate perspective is the contention that all literacies are, in fact, social, intertextual, and historical. The languages, cultures, literacy experiences, roles, and communities of readers and writers, as well as the immediate context, are critical influences on literacy development.

In the Psycholinguistic-Cognitive literature a second concept, interactivity, is most frequently defined as the interaction between reader and writer as the text is being processed.[13] In Socioliterate views, the concept of interactivity, like that of schemata, involves the larger culture in which readers, writers, and texts are found. Purves (1991, p. 63) tells us that this more inclusive understanding of the term assists students to develop strategies for processing discourses within a culture:

A reader in the United States . . . appears to know what texts are to be read for a single gist, or for the facts and procedures they detail. The reader knows, too, that certain texts that come in window envelopes with a first class stamp are bills, and others that come with window envelopes with cheaper postage are advertisements. A writer in the U.S. knows that a discursive composition is to be started with an anecdote or a generalization, and that a business letter should not include personal information. Each of these and more is a socially-approved act within a cultural context that is part of the textual contract determined by a sub-group in United States society.

Purves's comments are important for understanding expanded definitions of both interactivity and schemata. He is arguing for inclusion of the

---

13 Interactivity is also defined as the interaction between bottom-up processing of texts, at the sentence level, and top-down processing in which readers and writers rely on text macrostructures (see Grabe, 1988).

many and varied factors that tell us about a text in a genre and promote effective interactivity and processing. He is also arguing that literacies involve "socially-approved" acts, taking place within environments in which an informal and unstated contract exists between readers and writers. Successful text processing and production involves understanding the terms of this contact, terms that include text content, form, register, quality of paper, context, and many other factors. We understand and use texts because we are part of a community that accepts this contract as an efficient means for comprehending and producing particular written discourses. We read and write successfully because we work within the terms of the community contract. It should be noted, however, that the contract can be flexible, permitting considerable latitude, particularly for experienced, initiated readers and writers.

Integration of literacy views

In Figure 1, Socioliterate views, with their contextualized texts, are portrayed as central. As the figure indicates, however, these views are enriched by both of the theories discussed previously. From the Traditional, they draw upon the importance of form for all texts. In Socioliterate views, however, form is purpose-serving: It cannot be considered separately from the many other features of texts, roles, and contexts. The terms *schemata, interactivity,* and *processing* are taken from the Learner-Centered views and redefined for a Socioliterate perspective.

Before concluding this chapter, I must also discuss the downside of Socioliteracy, particularly the ways in which it, like all approaches, can be reduced or interpreted inappropriately. At least three inappropriate interpretations are discussed in the literature as Socioliterate practices become more common. The first is that teachers may view this paradigm shift as a return to Traditional practices, ignoring the social-constructionist elements and concentrating instead on text form as autonomous from the other factors that affect text processing and production. This reductionist approach is already appearing in some writing curricula in which rhetorical modes are again central. Another problem is that in promoting socioliteracies, teachers may neglect individual purposes and motivations and the creative ways in which readers and writers can work within social contracts. This must be avoided. Our students should not think of a social contract as a rigid set of rules, but as guidelines to be negotiated within specific contexts.

In the reading and writing of every text, there is a place for individual interpretations, purposes, and voices, and we should encourage students to experiment within, and outside, textual boundaries and conventions. Related to this point is the danger of teaching assimilation to academic

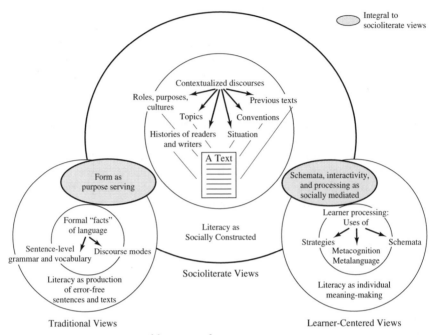

Figure 1   Integration of literacy theories.

cultures and their texts, rather than critique, of promoting students' acceptance of what is considered to be the status quo.[14] We must avoid this tendency by helping students to analyze, critique, and negotiate intelligently the texts, roles, and academic contexts in which they operate.

Applying a Socioliterate view is not easy, as this volume will indicate. As theories have evolved, from the Traditional to the Learner-Centered, and now to the Socioliterate, teaching and learning of literacies in first or second languages have been viewed as increasingly rich, demanding, complex, and multifaceted. Having taught within each of the major theoretical paradigms described here, I know that the Traditional is more limited, and thus easier to work within than the Learner-Centered. The Learner-Centered, at least as practiced in many reduced Process Approach classrooms, is easier and less inclusive than the Socioliterate approaches described in this volume. However, teaching and learning reading and writing practices cannot be simple or reductionist; there is no easy way. We practitioners must face reality, accept and even enjoy our demanding roles as teachers, learners, mediators, and researchers. Through our efforts, we can lay the foundation for developing literacy

14 Of course, because communities and texts are constantly changing, there may be no status quo.

practices that will continue through our students' academic and professional lives.

In our classrooms and on our campuses, we should assist students to draw from their past strategies and experiences and to develop new approaches to texts and tasks. Our classrooms should encourage student research into their own literacy and text histories, into current approaches to literate practices, and into strategies that work in a variety of contexts. We should encourage the investigation and critique of the literacy practices of others, particularly of more advanced students and faculty. Our classrooms should focus on variety, critical awareness, and analysis as we encourage students to become lifelong learners.

What I am advocating, then, is an approach in which literacy classes become laboratories for the study of texts, roles, and contexts, for research into evolving student literacies and developing awareness and critique of communities and their textual contracts. Our literacy classrooms can become places in which students are able to assess their current practices and understandings and develop strategies for future rhetorical situations. Though much can be accomplished in our classrooms, the full impact of the complexity of academic literacy cannot be felt without going outside and witnessing how literacy is practiced in other contexts. Kent tells us that "language-in-use . . . defies reduction to codifiable process or a system of logical relations" (1993, p. 3). This, of course, is the principal reason why students can begin, but not complete, their development of academic literacies in our classrooms.

2 Genre knowledge and socioliteracies
What readers and writers may share

Every time a student sits down to write for us, he has to invent the university for the occasion – invent the university, that is, or a branch of it, like History or Economics, or Anthropology or English. He has to learn to speak our language, to speak as we do, to try on the particular ways of knowing, selecting, evaluating, reporting, concluding and arguing that define the discourse of our community. Or perhaps I should say the various discourses of our community, since . . . a student . . . must work within fields where the rules governing the presentation of examples or the development of an argument are both distinct, and even to the professional, mysterious (Bartholomae, 1985, p. 134).

This comment from a famous essay on academic literacy underscores for us the dilemma faced by students when they attempt reading, writing, and other tasks within a variety of academic contexts.[1] As their literacy instructors, we must ask: "What is our role in helping students to solve academic 'mysteries'? What can we do to make students' academic literacy tasks more manageable? How can we assist them to 'invent' a text in a manner that is appropriate and personally satisfactory in academic contexts?"

Throughout this volume, I argue that we can prepare students for approaching challenging academic texts and tasks by asking them to review what they already know and to assess current rhetorical situations in light of that knowledge. In this chapter I discuss one important intellectual resource that students bring with them to our classrooms – their knowledge of "genre." Since genre knowledge is central to a socioliterate pedagogy, I will begin by presenting some general issues and then discuss these issues as they apply to academic contexts.

The following questions will be addressed in this chapter:

1. What knowledge do readers and writers who communicate using texts from a genre appear to share? What common understandings do they seem to have?
2. What are the implications of this sharing for our classrooms?

---

1 See McCarthy (1987) and Walvoord and McCarthy (1990) for rich and useful studies of student attempts to "invent the university."

Throughout the chapter, I maintain that frequent review and reflection upon genre knowledge can assist students in developing a rich understanding of texts that can serve them throughout their academic and professional lives.

Traditionally, the term *genre* has referred to categories of literary texts. For many years, students in literature classrooms have been assigned to read texts referred to as "novels," "poems," or "epics" as examples from genres. Recently, however, the term has been employed to refer to much more: to varieties of expository prose, to types of films, and to musical categories.[2] Whatever the topic, there appear to be certain understandings between speakers (or writers) and listeners (or readers) about the characteristics of the particular genre being discussed.

Because this volume is devoted primarily to literacy, the focus of this chapter will be on written discourses.[3] Before beginning this discussion, it is important to emphasize that an individual's genre knowledge is abstract and schematic, enhanced by repeated, contextualized experiences with texts. Schematic memories of a genre can initially be "fuzzy" (Swales, 1993), or even contradictory, because experiences with texts may be passing, partially remembered, or inconsistent. As people become experienced readers and writers, however, they begin to work more easily within familiar genres. They are able to separate texts into genre categories in order to assist themselves, and other readers and writers, in identifying, processing, and remembering textual experiences. Thus, as individuals have repeated, situated experiences with texts from a genre category, their schematic memories of these texts and relevant contexts become increasingly reliable. They are able to identify texts by a community-designated name, and read, comprehend, and perhaps write similar texts with increasing ease and effectiveness. Genre knowledge provides a shortcut for the initiated to the processing and production of familiar written texts.

An individual's abstract genre knowledge is both complex and dichotomous. It is, at the same time, cognitive (integral to schemata, or prior knowledge) and social (shared with other readers and writers who have experienced the genre). It is "repeated" (Miller, 1984) in that it evokes previous, analogous contexts in which similar texts were processed; yet it is evolving (Berkenkotter & Huckin, 1995), because few, if any, rhetorical situations are exactly the same. Genre knowledge is systematic (Bhatia, 1993; Kay, 1993) and conventional, in that form and

2 One of my Japanese students told me that the word *genre* has been borrowed into her language. In Japanese, it is also used to refer to types of music or films as well as to literary genres.
3 Discussing types of films and music as genres in the classroom can be quite useful, however, because many of today's students are more musically or cinematically than textually experienced.

style may be repeated. Yet a person's knowledge of conventions, to be useful, must be open to change (Kent, 1993, p. 128), constantly subject to revision as situations are transformed. When discussing genres, then, we are discussing complex, evolving mental abstractions held by individuals within communities or larger cultures who share social and textual experiences. All literate people have genre knowledge: of "homely" discourses (Miller, 1984) such as recipes; of sacred texts, such as the *Koran;* of political texts, such as ballots; of pedagogical texts, such as school essays. We must draw from our own genre knowledge, and that of our students and colleagues, to assist us in understanding what it means to be literate in academic and professional contexts.

What do those with a common knowledge of a genre share? What is said to be stored in memory or understood about a particular genre that will assist experienced readers and writers to process and produce effective texts from that genre? Theorists and researchers suggest that some, or all, of the following can be found among those who share knowledge of a genre.

A shared name

It is a human trait to name and categorize, and for those who share genre knowledge within a culture, there is generally a shared name. People who read, teach, or study literature speak of "a novel," "a poem," or "a mystery." Anthropologists have also employed shared names to identify categories of discourses. Early in this century, for example, Sapir (1909) spoke of "myths," "letters," and "nonmythical narratives" as discourse types deserving of classification and study (see also Swales, 1990, pp. 34– 36). There has been considerable discussion of genre naming (and use) among educators and applied linguists as well (see, for example, Chapman, 1994; Freedman & Medway, 1994a).

In the academic communities to which we literacy faculty belong, we may share genre knowledge of "an abstract" or "a critical review" in publications in our disciplines, particularly if we have consistently read or written texts from these genres. Our experienced students have names for their familiar pedagogical genres as well. Mine, for example, speak of "a book report" and "a five-paragraph essay," two genres that are frequently assigned in their classes.

Thus experienced readers and writers tend to share names for categories of written texts.[4] These communally held names provide a kind of

4 Unfortunately, naming can vary considerably, even among those individuals who are considered to be in the same discourse community. In their ambitious survey of

shorthand for identifying texts and the situations in which they occur. In cultures outside academia, people identify by name types of "homely texts" (Miller, 1984) such as "the thank-you note." They can name humorous discourses such as "the parody," "the pastiche," "the impersonation," or "the send-up" (Swales, 1993). If they are from specialized communities, such as law, they may share names of professional genre categories, such as "the court order." It is convenient and efficient for people to share names of texts, for this practice enables them to begin their reading and writing of a text with considerable confidence and to comprehend effectively the discourses that are important to them.

When a name is shared, it evokes in experienced readers and writers certain expectations: for particular features or conventions of the text, for certain reader and writer roles, and for specific contexts in which the texts are found. However, the name can mean much more than that, for shared naming is important to an understanding of the central purposes that texts serve within communities of readers and writers. Swales has found that "a discourse community's nomenclature for genres is an important source of insight" (1990, p. 54) into community values and "ways of being in the world" (Geertz, 1983, p. 155). To illustrate his point, Swales lists names of presentation categories taken from an applied linguistics conference program (1990, p. 56). These include "basic presentations," "*haiku* presentations," "experimental workshops," and "creative workshops." He speculates that the conference organizers and presenters undoubtedly had specific and quite different purposes for these presentations, purposes that affect form, language, presentation style, length, and topic, among other factors.

Some genres, particularly in pedagogical contexts, are loosely, and almost casually, named. When a faculty member assigns a "research paper," for example, it is difficult for students to determine from the name what is required. The problem with defining and classifying this particular text category is further exacerbated by the teaching of "the research paper" as a specific, fixed text type in many literacy classes. In an effort to counteract this practice, Larson (1982) argues, quite convincingly, that research may be reported in many kinds of texts; thus, there is no one "research paper" genre that applies to all classrooms:

Research can inform virtually any writing or speaking if the author wishes it to do so; there is nothing of substance or content that differentiates one paper that draws on data from outside the author's own self from another such paper – nothing that can enable one to say that this paper is a "research paper" and that paper is not . . . I would assert therefore that the so-called

Brazilian businesses, for example, Barbara et al. (1996) found that different businesses use different names, such as "bids" and "reports," for what appear to be texts in the same genre.

"research paper," as a generic, cross-disciplinary term, has no conceptual or substantive identity (p. 813).

Unfortunately for us, and for our students, the same claims can be made about other pedagogical genres. What is an "in-class essay" for example? What can we say about its organization, its stylistic conventions, or its length? What is a "take-home examination"? What is a "study summary"? Thus, though naming can be central to understanding how genre knowledge is realized purposefully in some academic and "homely" contexts, we must also contend in our literacy classrooms with the casual naming of pedagogical texts by discipline-specific (DS) faculty,[5] and the difficulties that this practice poses for students who are seeking guidance. DS faculty often complain that the most common question addressed to them by students about an assignment is "What do you want?" Although the students may not know how to pose questions about texts or tasks, their concerns are valid, because each faculty member may have a considerably different understanding of the purposes, form, and content of the pedagogical text he or she has assigned.

Despite these considerable obstacles, we can still use naming to begin a discussion of texts. If our students are encouraged to ask faculty questions such as "What does a 'research paper' mean to you? How would you organize a research paper? Do you have examples papers written for your classes?" they have begun their own research into the socioliterate practices of their instructors and the academic communities with which the faculty identify. And, not incidentally, they have begun to understand the specific constraints of the assignments for their classes.

Shared communicative purposes

Naming of genres is often closely related to purpose or intentionality. In most situations, readers and writers use texts purposefully to communicate with others. Because purpose is an important consideration, genres have often been categorized according to the particular jobs they are said to accomplish. A sales letter is said to persuade readers to buy; a funeral oration is most often intended to honor the deceased; a recipe instructs the reader about cooking a dish. However, we need to be very careful about attributing single purposes to texts from a genre. As we know from *Julius Caesar,* Mark Antony had multiple purposes in mind for his funeral oration; sales letters may be intended to introduce a company to a client; recipes can provide ways for the writers to preen before their intended

---

5 *Discipline-specific faculty* are those identified with a single discipline, an area of study that generally has a few standard textbooks, recognized journals, and, in many cases, a predictable department name. History, literature, economics, biology, chemistry, and engineering are traditional disciplines, for example.

audiences. In academic and professional genres, the writers' purposes can also be several. Bhatia (1993) tells us, for example, that in the academic research article, discourses with two apparent purposes appear almost immediately: the abstract and the introduction. He argues that the basic social purpose for the abstract is to summarize the entire article; however, the purpose for the introduction is to draw the reader into the text. As this example illustrates, we need to be very careful about attributing single purposes to texts, or to writers – or readers – for that matter.

In Australia, where genre-related pedagogies are well developed, particularly in primary, secondary, and adult schools, the purposes that texts are purported to serve are some of the first topics discussed in the classroom (see Derewianka, 1990). A few purposeful text categories identified for teaching in Australia are "procedure" (how something is done), "description" (what some particular thing is like), "report" (what an entire class of things is like), "explanation" (a reason why a judgment is made), and "argument" (why a thesis has been produced) (Richardson, 1994). Some practitioners view this formal categorization by purpose, language, and form as a return to the Traditional approaches discussed in Chapter 1, thus limiting students' understanding of the complexities of genres. Others, acknowledging the importance of form in understanding and producing texts, maintain that terms such as "explanation," "argument," and "description" relate to some of the many strategies for completing discourses across genres (see Kiniry & Rose, 1993). Whatever their theoretical stance, those who focus on the social construction of texts tend to agree that exploring purposes of writers (and readers) is important to student development of genre knowledge.

One central point made by genre theorists and pedagogues in Australia and elsewhere is that purpose interacts with features of text at every discourse level. If a writer's purposes are to be accomplished, then he or she should be aware of the forms, argumentation, and content that have become conventional in the tradition of a genre. Experts argue that with this background, a writer can manipulate appropriate conventions more effectively to achieve communicative purposes within a particular context.

Shared knowledge of roles

Genre knowledge also requires literate individuals to consider the social roles of readers and writers as they are realized within texts and contexts. Roles relate, first of all, to purpose. In some types of business letters, for example, the writer initiates the text and takes the more forceful role of complainer or requester, and the reader is the one who must deal politely with the complaint or decide how to respond to the request. In academic research articles, where readers and writers are generally peers, the writers may argue or explain and the readers comprehend and critique. Individual and social purposes and role relationships are complex, of course, but their relationships to text and contexts provide important and interesting topics for classroom discussion. In one of my classes, for example, we examined a collection of "first-person accounts," a common genre in history. Each of the texts dealt with the same topic, the Nazi concentration camps, yet the text writers, a commandant, a prisoner, and an American soldier, had considerably different roles (and purposes) in producing their texts. The class discussed what these roles and purposes might be and how they influenced the content and argumentation in the texts. From this discussion, the students realized that role plays an important part in purpose, and both purpose and role affect how a text is written or read.

Roles are also related to the complicated issues of power and authority. When a judge issues "a court order," he or she not only has considerable power over the text but over those who are intended to read it: the lawyers, the defendants, and the plaintiffs. In other contexts, it is the readers who hold the power. Those reviewing grant proposals or articles for publication hold considerable power over the writers, as many of us know. In most academic classrooms, it is the DS faculty who hold the power, because it is they who write the curricula, establish the assignments and examinations, and grade the students. Faculty organize and present material, often in lecture form, and they set the examinations. Students ask questions, and on rare occasions may be able to negotiate their assignments, but they are seldom able to negotiate class content or grades. In some parts of the world, students view this power relationship as adversarial, "students vs. teacher" (Muchiri et al., 1995, p. 181). Thus, the students work together to "beat the system," particularly the examinations, where what might be called "cheating" in the United States is seen by these students as group resistance to a hierarchy over which they have no control. In literacy classrooms throughout the world, the relationship between students and teachers is usually less adversarial, because instructors are concerned with literacy growth and student motivation. However, in almost every classroom, including the Expressivist, it is the teacher who makes the important rules and assigns the grades.

Power, status, and purpose cannot tell the full story about the complexity of role relationships, however. We must also consider the background knowledge of the readers and writers, their shared (or unshared) values and statuses, and their previous interactions. There is the degree of intimacy to consider, for sometimes we write to those we love; and, at other times, we write (or read the writing of) those we have never met. Computers have brought to our discourses a very interesting panoply of role relationships. On the Internet, individuals begin and end romances with people they have never seen or write to unknown colleagues within interest groups in a familiar manner.

Like all of the features of genre knowledge discussed here, role interacts with the processing and production of texts at a number of levels. Thus we cannot separate reader and writer roles from our studies of genre name, from purpose, from context, from conventions, or from other factors that contribute to the processing and production of texts.

Shared knowledge of context

How do writers or readers identify texts by name and establish their purposes and reader and writer roles? One way is to recognize recurring features of the context, the "sphere of human activity" (Bakhtin, 1986, p. 65) in which texts from an identified genre are being repeatedly produced and processed. Context refers not merely to a physical place, such as a classroom, or a particular publication, such as a journal, but to all of the nonlinguistic and nontextual elements that contribute to the situation in which reading and writing are accomplished. Thus, context refers to "the events that are going on around when people speak [and write]" (Halliday, 1991, p. 5).

Many contextual elements reoccur in our life experience. We return to publications, events, and places that are identified with familiar discourses, over and over again. In my family, for example, we often attend plays; therefore, we are quite familiar with the genre we call "a playbill." We spend considerable time in the kitchen; therefore, we are comfortable with recipes. We are inveterate newspaper readers, so we are comfortable with editorials and comic strips. When a text appears in a familiar context, individuals can draw upon their prior genre knowledge to develop a plan for dealing with the current textual demands. This is true in our professional lives as well. After we have presented at a conference, for example, we are usually able to present again in a conference context with a certain amount of sophistication. This phenomenon is also apparent in our students' academic literacy lives. My science students have written several "lab reports" in science classrooms, so they are not complete novices when a lab report is again assigned in a classroom context. For Brown et al. (1989), this knowledge of past contexts and their genres is a kind of situated cognition, a sense of text that is transferred to comparable contexts. Because of this potential for transfer, Halliday suggests that students be asked to "predict both ways; to predict the text from the context, and to predict the context from the text" (Halliday, 1991, p. 22).

Students' situated cognition will undoubtedly become more and more sophisticated as they repeatedly recognize contexts in which texts from a particular genre are required. By repeating (and revising) the conventions of a genre and by practicing context analysis, students can learn what are "situationally appropriate generic behaviors" (Berkenkotter & Huckin, 1995, p. 8). It would be advisable, then, to help our students to reflect on their previous experiences with texts from a genre and on their already-acquired situated cognition, thus enabling them to approach future text experiences in analogous contexts with increasing confidence.

Misdirected situated cognition can present major problems for our students, however, if they apply to a current situation all of the strategies and text understandings that they applied to previous, apparently analogous ones. Why? Because the expectations for an "in-class essay examination" for one class may be quite different from those of another. A "research paper" for one class, as Benson (1996) and Larson (1982) have noted, may vary in many ways from those required in the students' previous classes. It is often difficult for students to determine what elements of a text should be repeated from the previous, apparently analogous context, and what elements must be revised to meet the needs of the current situation. In explaining this dilemma, Berkenkotter and Huckin (1995, after Bakhtin, 1981) speak of the *centripetal forces* that contribute to text prototypicality in apparently similar contexts and, conversely, to the *centrifugal forces* in a specific situation that require variation in text processing and production. They warn that "recurring situations resemble each other only in certain ways and only to a certain degree" (1995, p. 6). The reader's or writer's task is to apply to the current situation those strategies and understandings that are appropriate, and to discard, at least temporarily, those that are not.

Kent tells us that processing a text for a particular context marks "the place along the chain of communicative interaction where the passing theory [of genre] takes concrete form" (1993, p. 167). He maintains that genre knowledge must always be considered an "open system" for individuals' understandings and that situated cognition should be in a constant state of revision. Individual literacy theories must be perpetually evolving as readers and writers confront "new," yet in some ways repeated, rhetorical contexts and demands (p. 167).

Thus our students often have trouble dealing with the centripetal and centrifugal forces that are inherent in effective academic reading and writing. As a result, they may attempt to simplify their theories of genre and thus their assigned tasks. My students, for example, insist that I must help them to discover *one* way to structure in-class essay examinations, hoping that they will be able to impose their unrevised knowledge of this pedagogical genre on all future academic situations. They frequently ask questions about texts such as, "Don't we always write the thesis sentence at the end of the first paragraph? Don't we always use semicolons before 'however'? Don't we always divide texts into five paragraphs?" The answer, of course, is "there is no *always*. . . , but there are some times!" Encouraging students to balance what they have learned from previous contexts with the demands of the current situation is one of our chief responsibilities. We must urge students to draw from past experiences yet not become slaves to them, to revise what they already know for the situation at hand. In order to carry out this responsibility, we should "insist that each piece of writing – or reading – we assign have a specifically defined rhetorical situation" (Coe, 1993).[6] In addition, we need to provide students with differing textual experiences constrained by various roles, purposes, and contexts.

Shared knowledge of formal text features (conventions)

What can students draw from as they confront an academic situation in which they are required to read or write a text? What information from past experiences with texts can be useful for them? In addition to the points mentioned above, genre knowledge must include a sense of text form, because in many cases there are formal characteristics of a genre that members of a community have come to expect, features that enable community members to read and write with confidence. Some genres are viewed as "highly structured and conventionalized" (Bhatia, 1993, p. 14) by those who read and write them frequently. My graduate linguistics students, when exploring genres in their first or second languages, have found that newspaper obituaries in some cultures (Japan; Kishida, 1995) and court orders in other cultures (the United States; January, 1995) may fit into this category. My undergraduate science and engineering students claim that they have memorized the sentence syntax and discourse structure required of every lab report. Because of spoken, or unspoken, agreements among the DS faculty, the formal features of texts in this genre do not appear to vary considerably from class to class, nor (the students claim) have the genre requirements varied much since the mid-1980s. On the other hand, there are pedagogical genres whose formal features are almost completely unpredictable, a problem that I have already mentioned.

6 For Coe, and for most rhetoricians, the "rhetorical situation" includes several of the genre categories I have mentioned here. He argues that students should always be asking these questions:
  1. What am I (are we) trying to accomplish? (Purpose)
  2. With whom? (Audience)
  3. Under what circumstances and in what genre? (Occasion)

Formal features can refer to the macrostructure of an entire text. Text macrostructure can be indicated by headings ("Introduction," "Methodology," "Results"), by particular phrases ("We can conclude from this study, then . . . "), or by other conventions. There are also formal discourse features within one section of a longer text, often called "moves." Swales's famous CARS model of moves in research paper introductions (1981, 1990) serves as an important example of this phenomenon. Swales and others have found that writers of research articles tend to make four purposeful moves in the discourse of an introduction, enabling experienced readers to process this section rapidly and efficiently. These moves are as follows.

Move 1: Establishing the research field (introducing the topic, discussing its importance).
Move 2: Summarizing previous research (a short review of the important literature).
Move 3: Preparing for present research (showing the "gap" between previous research and the focus of the particular the study under discussion).
Move 4: Introducing the present research (stating the purpose of the study under discussion).

Recently, Connor has expanded and refined the discussion of moves within other academic genres, such as the grant proposal (1996, pp. 132–135).

Socially influenced conventions can appear at lower levels of text as well. Like formal features at every level, sentence syntax or other grammatical choices are often purposeful and community-driven. For example, there appear to be historical and disciplinary reasons why noun compounding is characteristic of the sciences (Halliday & Martin, 1993) and why the passive is used to serve various purposes in certain scientific texts (Tarone et al., 1981). There also appear to be historical and cultural reasons why complex conjunctions are absent from most American English business letters (Johns, 1981a).

Thus, form at all levels of written texts cannot be considered separately from other genre characteristics, for these elements often serve the repeated, social purposes of a genre. Kay (1993, p. 10) argues that form contributes to what we consider to be conventional, or generic, for particular contexts:

[Genres] have conventional forms because of the situations they arise in, and the knowledge of what has gone before. What is appropriate and what affects certain actuation are likely to lead people to respond in similar ways – thus the *conventions* are established and begin to repeat themselves.

I have argued here that form, whether it be in the global organization of the text (macrostructure), in its various divisions or sections (moves), or in its sentence-level elements, can serve generic purposes within contexts and among communities of readers and writers. Formal features are not ends in themselves but means for achieving particular ends. Thus we should not teach forms separately, but should encourage students to view formal features as integral to understanding a genre.

It is important to note that text form within a genre category is seldom, if ever, stable, despite what my students may claim about lab reports or wish were true about other pedagogical genres. There is a growing literature showing that genres evolve and decay at all formal levels over time. Perhaps "evolve" is not always the appropriate term, for there may be a powerful agent who is instrumental in initiating these changes. Discussing scientific genres, Berkenkotter and Huckin (1995, p. 39) note, for example, that the ordinary scientific writer can institute only minor changes in the forms of published research; a journal editor, however, may take a more powerful role:

[W]hatever rhetorical moves scientists can make to get the attention of their readership will have to be small ones, done discreetly within conventionalized formats currently in use . . . only *powerful journal editors* [emphasis added] are in a position to change the existing genre conventions in any major way.

Thus we can say that in addition to genre name, role identification, and context, shared experiences with formal features of texts can assist readers and writers in meeting the demands of a particular rhetorical situation. These features can be exploited to forward the writer's own, and the community's, purposes, to argue, to show solidarity or demonstrate disagreement. Though situations (and formal features of texts) are seldom if ever repeated in every detail, experienced individuals draw from past genre knowledge of form to plan, draft, and revise texts – or to read them intelligently.

Shared knowledge of text content

Consideration of text content and how it interacts with other features is essential to a comprehensive understanding of genre knowledge. Berkenkotter and Huckin (1995, p. 14) argue that "what constitutes true genre knowledge is not just knowledge of formal conventions but a knowledge of appropriate topics and relevant details as well." The types of content and vocabulary that are brought into the text, the ways in which the content is organized, the assumptions about prior knowledge of readers and about appropriate use of details are all essential to sophisticated knowledge of a genre within a discipline. Though form has received much more attention than content in genre research and pedagogy, some content studies have been completed, especially on scientific research genres. Huckin (1987), for example, found that in biology articles from a selected journal, titles have become more informative over time, often including mention not only of topic but of methodology and results. The introductions in this journal now include information about results. On the other hand, the methodology sections have been shortened over the past few years. Huckin concludes from this study that form may be more conventionalized and slower to change than content; it is content that may have altered the nature of the scientific research article over the past 20 years or so (Berkenkotter & Huckin, 1995).

Giltrow and Valiquette (1994) conducted another study of content that can be useful to our understanding. Arguing that "genre [is] a system for administering communities' knowledge of the world – a system for housing knowledge and producing and practicing it" (p. 47), these authors asked experienced teaching assistants from the disciplines of psychology and criminology to read novice students' papers and comment on their abilities to manage disciplinary knowledge. After reviewing the teaching assistants' comments, the researchers concluded that the way knowledge is managed differs considerably between the two disciplines. In psychology, student writers are required to demonstrate an understanding of how to manage detail, "to make numerous judgments about what to mention and what to keep quiet about" (p. 51). In criminology, on the other hand, students had to "handle concepts from the heart of criminological reasoning" (p. 53). The researchers concluded that "the disciplines display or conceal insider knowledge in elaborate (and different) ways" (p. 58), a useful statement for us to explore with our students and faculty colleagues.

Content presents many difficult challenges to students. One that they face when writing a text is deciding what content to include and what to leave out, what the reader(s) already know that need not be repeated and what must be mentioned. In their introductory academic classes, much of the content that students include in their written texts is already known by their instructors, so they have considerable problems making these decisions. Their DS professors already know all of the information, and the students worry that they may not want to read it again. But if the students don't write about what their professors know, how can they demonstrate that they understand it? Students also face difficulties related to content in reading: relating what they read to what they have read previously, understanding the concepts of disciplinary practice, and comprehending the vocabulary as it is used in a discipline. Many students argue that content, especially vocabulary understanding, is their greatest obstacle to developing academic literacies.

Shared register

Register refers to the predominance of particular lexical and grammatical feature categories within a genre. It is one of the most important elements in what we might call "style" or "text conventions." Years ago, Halliday, McIntosh, and Strevens defined register as purposeful: "language varies as its function varies; it differs in different situations. The name given to a variety of language distinguished according to its use is register" (1964, p. 87). The most obvious and the most frequently taught features of academic registers are the concentrations of vocabulary related to particular disciplines. We still see in many literacy and English for Specific Purposes textbooks lists of common technical words for students to learn. However, in discussing genre knowledge, it is important to go beyond these lists and consider how vocabulary serves the values and communicative purposes of readers, writers, and communities. In making this point, Halliday (1993) speaks of the interlocking nature of scientific vocabularies and their relationships to *conceptual taxonomies*. He argues that if students study core vocabulary appropriately, they can begin to understand the basic values, concepts, organizational preferences, and taxonomies of a discipline. In a case study of a first-year university student enrolled in an anthropology class, I made the same discovery (Johns, 1992). This successful ESL student organized her vocabulary study around the concepts of her anthropology class, learning the terms as they related to specific examples. Her notes were arranged into concept trees, and thus her study was both meaningful and appropriate to the taxonomies of the class content. She reported that her approach to vocabulary and concept study was useful in many classes, assisting her in attaining consistently high grades.

In addition to vocabulary, grammatical concentrations in texts have been central to our understanding of register. The text analysis literature of the past 20 years or so, particularly in English for Specific Purposes (see Swales, 1988a; Bhatia, 1993) and contrastive rhetoric (see Connor, 1996), is replete with studies of grammatical feature concentrations in certain types of texts.[7] Researchers have examined the concentrations of particular forms of verbs, the predominance of modals in various texts, and many other features. These findings are useful to literacy practitioners; however, register features must be considered with other genre elements, not independently from the social purposes of texts, reader and writer roles, and contexts.

---

7 It is important to note that concordancing and other computer-aided text research has contributed significantly to our understanding of register (see, for example, Biber et al., 1996; Finegan, 1996). In the United States, much of this work has been inspired by Doug Biber at Northern Arizona University.

Shared cultural values

Perhaps the most interesting and challenging discussions in genre studies relate to the shared cultural values of readers and writers of texts within a genre, the "ways of being in the world" (Geertz, 1983) of particular groups or communities of readers and writers. In discussing their famous hypothesis, Sapir and Whorf argued for a theory that encompasses the interplay of language, shared life experiences, and values (Whorf, 1956). Related views of cultures and communities and their involvement with language and genres will be discussed in Chapter 3.

Interviews with DS faculty over the years have led me to conclude that most tend to believe there is a single set of academic values shared by all academic disciplines. Some argue that all educated people share the values that are central to academic literacy: good writing, effective reading, careful listening and note taking, and sound critical thinking. When I conducted writing-across-the-curriculum workshops, I discovered that most faculty believe quite sincerely that literacy instructors can teach students some generalized approaches to each of these academic values, which will serve the students in every context and disciplinary culture. As a result, faculty complain to us when their students "can't read and write" the types of texts assigned in their classrooms. What these faculty don't realize, of course, is that "good writing" in a literature class may not be considered "good writing" in a business class; in fact, I have taught business writing to creative writing students who have earned low grades because they can write only in one register. In addition, "effective reading" for one purpose does not serve another; the way we read novels is not the way we read computer documentation, for example. How one listens and takes notes will depend on the context and the manner in which a lecture is delivered. Thus, we can discuss general academic values only in a very general way (see Chapter 4).

Different "critical thinking" demands are also difficult to explain to faculty, many of whom insist that this is a single, teachable "skill," separate from the content, concepts, and values of disciplines. Considerable research evidence demonstrates that these faculty are, for the most part, misguided. There are those who are excellent critical thinkers in one discipline, such as computer science, but who have considerable trouble thinking critically in another, such as history. Our university admits talented literature students who must take "remedial" mathematics because they fail the entrance test requiring critical thinking using mathematical formulas.

One of our many responsibilities as literacy practitioners is to prepare our students, and our faculty colleagues, to explore the values that drive literacies in their classes and communities. For both groups, these explorations can be educational. They can assist faculty in considering how they might discuss good reading or writing, what it means to think critically in their disciplines, and how notes or examinations might be taken in the classes that they teach. Those explorations can assist students to become researchers in each of their academic classrooms, to vary their literacy approaches depending on the class content, the texts, and the disciplinary context.

More will be said about cultural values and how they influence literacy practices and ideologies throughout the volume. Here, I will only note that values as realized in texts are important to genre knowledge.

Shared awareness of intertextuality

Finally, there is the issue of intertextuality. As can be seen from the discussion earlier in this chapter, expert readers and writers of texts from a genre share "repeated" contexts, text names, and analogous experiences with reader and writer roles, text form, and content. What they experience with a particular text in a specific rhetorical situation is mediated through their past text experiences. For these reasons, then, "genre cannot be fruitfully characterized as a facet of the immanent properties of particular texts . . . [for] genre is quintessentially intertextual" (Briggs & Baumann, 1992, p. 147).

Widdowson tells us that "no text is an island" (1993, p. 27). Certainly not: Individual texts are influenced by previous experiences of all kinds, with texts of the same genre and with texts and spoken discourses from outside the genre. Experienced readers and writers draw from their previous genre knowledge and experiences to process a text within a specific context. In every discipline, experienced writers defend or reject hypotheses, methods, theories, and practices they have read about in other texts. In their classes, students' essay examination responses generally refer to the assigned readings, lectures, and discussions. The students' textbooks are also highly intertextual, drawing from the literature in the discipline and often from other textbooks.

We can safely say that every academic text draws from and depends on other texts and discoursal experiences in some way, and thus is intertextual. How former experiences with texts are exploited for the production of new ones will depend on the task, the writer's purposes, reader and writer roles, the context, and several other factors. In one case, genre conventions may be "reproduced" from past discourses (Berkenkotter & Huckin, 1995, p. 17); for example, writers may follow the CARS model for moves in article introductions (Swales, 1990), which they have seen in similar texts. In another case, a writer's argumentation is strengthened through the citation of an authority drawn from a volume taken from the library. For other texts, writers draw from data gathered in laboratories or through interviews. The list of possibilities for intertextual influences on texts is infinite. When discussing the complexity of intertextuality, Briggs and Baumann note that "structure, form, function and meaning are . . . seen as products of an ongoing process of producing and receiving discourse" (1992, p. 146).

What does this persuasive intertextuality in genres mean for our students in academic classes? How does intertextuality affect their understandings of genres and their evolving literacies? On the content level, students must realize that

> . . . any single piece of college writing is part of an ongoing written discussion about a topic, and . . . [students] are expected to make a contribution to that discussion.
> Writers participate in the discussion by acknowledging other perspectives or points of view, or by identifying the content which gives rise to their own arguments (Fitzgerald, 1988, p. 63).

Like the other features of genre, intertextuality provides an excellent discussion topic for the literacy classroom. Students can discuss their reliance on their lecture notes, conversations, experiments, and classroom readings in writing their texts. They can talk about how observations or library sources influenced their argumentation. They can mention their previous experiences with form in a genre. Students can also focus on their intertextual experiences outside the classroom. In one of my classes, for example, we discussed the intertextual experiences of the president of our department's student association. She had decided to write a memo to the department faculty requesting that they give presentations at the annual colloquium. Though this student president had had some experiences with memos and with addressing the faculty, she identified a number of problems she needed to solve before drafting her text, including the ordering of her moves, and making decisions about register and the force of her argumentation. Intertextuality continuously entered her writing process. In addition to consulting memos written by previous club presidents on this topic, she had conversations with key members of the faculty before writing her first draft. She revised, then took this copy to other faculty for comment. Her text "dialogued" with numerous faculty at various points in its creation long before the final version appeared in faculty mailboxes. In this example, conversations and analogous texts were the intertextual discourses that most influenced the student's document. However, when producing other types of discourses, students use references or observed data to enhance a text's intertextuality. Experiences such as these can be considered when we discuss developing reading abilities, enhancing writing processes, and producing effective written products.

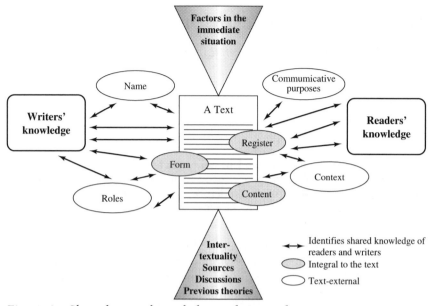

Figure 1   Shared genre knowledge and situated cognition.

In this chapter, I have discussed what readers and writers may share when they communicate using texts from a genre. Figure 1 shows the potential features of shared knowledge discussed in this chapter – knowledge that can contribute to an individual's situated cognition. A reader's or writer's knowledge of a text name, the conventional roles of readers and writers of a text in this genre, standard purposes, context, content, values, and intertextuality can result in efficient and effective processing of a text. When student readers share some or all of this knowledge with the writer of an assigned text, they comprehend, and we are happy with their text summaries. When writers share this knowledge, readers are often pleased with their ability to produce what is considered appropriate written products. This sharing makes reading and writing much more efficient, and it contributes to mutual understanding among those involved. Without it, the lives of readers and writers would be much more difficult because they would have to make many more decisions before processing each text. Because some of our students do *not* share academic genre knowledge with their instructors, or with other readers and writers, they face considerable obstacles. It is these obstacles that we should attempt to face in our socioliterate curricula.

3 Genre and social forces
"Homely" and academic texts

The most important lesson for student writers to learn is that genres are socially real and that to participate effectively in a discourse community, one usually must adapt to (or around) readers' generic expectations. Students should learn to notice genres, to make sense of genres, and even to renovate genres (Coe, 1994, p. 165).

In the previous chapter it was suggested that considering texts as examples of genres encourages the study not only of the structure and content of written discourses, but of how these internal textual elements interact with other texts and social and cultural forces in particular contexts. In this chapter some of these social and cultural forces are discussed. Using familiar examples of genres, I first note some of the interactions between culture and text. Then, I turn to academic texts, professional faculty genres, and a genre more familiar to students, the textbook. By using these varied examples of texts realized through shared knowledge, I shall demonstrate why a discussion of the social construction of texts is vital to the classroom.

In this chapter, I will discuss the following questions:

1. How can practitioners use "homely" discourses to introduce students to concepts of genres and to the social forces that influence situated texts?
2. What are some of the features of professional faculty genres that can influence academic classrooms?
3. How can we encourage the study of pedagogical genres, especially the textbook, in promoting the development of socioliteracies?

"Homely" texts

In this section, I will discuss genres that should be familiar to all readers of this volume, named texts that cross linguistic and cultural lines. These genres are not high-flown or literary; instead, they are what Miller (1984) calls "homely" discourses, the texts of everyday life. If we assist our students in viewing the homely texts around them as genre exemplars, and thus socially constructed, we can enable them to view academic discourses as socially constructed as well.

The wedding invitation

When we analyze genres, we should attempt to examine more than one text, thereby assisting students in hypothesizing about what is repeated from other texts and what has been revised for a particular context. A collection of texts that I have brought to conferences in several parts of the world is from the genre called the "wedding invitation."

Figure 1 shows invitations in two different languages (English and Spanish), both of which have been immediately identified by name. After displaying the texts and asking for their genre name, I pose this question to audiences: "Why do you know that these are wedding invitations? What is it about these two texts that cause us to place them in the same category?" Generally, the audiences identify two areas of genre knowledge that provide clues: content and form. In wedding invitations, the predictable content includes the mention of "wedding" or "marriage," the names of the bride and groom, and the time and place of the ceremony. The phrasal form in which each element of the invitation appears on a separate line is also conventionalized. In some texts, there are nonlinguistic clues as well: decorations and borders with wedding symbols (bells, bow, hearts).[1] These text features assist experienced readers and writers in immediately identifying texts from the genre.

Another element of genre knowledge is also attributed to these texts by audiences: communicative purpose. Families prepare and send wedding invitations to include others in their marriage celebrations. However, as is the case for most genres, there may be other, more implicit purposes, as well: to fulfill social obligations, to demonstrate wealth or status, or to announce that the couple is finally "tying the knot." Thus, in the case of wedding invitations, shared name, communicative purpose(s), and specific elements of content and form are often carried over from one "repeated" (Miller, 1984) situation to another across languages and national boundaries. Experienced readers and writers throughout the world have developed a wedding invitation schema, and with it, they recognize a genre exemplar.

It is also immediately apparent that the two invitations in Figure 1 are different from each other in important ways. In the English text, there is no mention of the names of the parents, an issue that was negotiated between the bride and groom and their families. In the other text, and in most other wedding invitations, the names of both sets of parents are mentioned. My informants from various countries tell me that the ap-

---

1 Some Indonesian invitations are also scented!

Together with their families

Barbara Elizabeth Johns

and

Kevin Blair Howard

request the honor of your presence
at their marriage
on Saturday, the seventh of January
nineteen hundred and ninety-five
at four-thirty in the afternoon
United Church of Christ of La Mesa
5940 Kelton Avenue
La Mesa, California

Lorraine y Mario Rodríguez   Norma y Francisco García

Les participan el enlace matrimonial de sus hijos

Monique Rodríguez R. y Francisco García M.

Y tienen el honor de invitarlos a la misa nupcial que se celebrará a las

5:00 de la tarde el
viernes 19 de mayo de 1993 en
Holy Spirit Catholic Church
2755 55th Street
San Diego, California

Recepción 6:30 a 12:00, The Bristol Court Hotel, 1055 First Avenue

Padrinos

Velación: Frances y Gilbert Gutiérrez
Anillos: Ma. Ysabelle Rodríguez Ch. y Daniel Chong-Jiménez

Lazo: Lyále Montes Ch. y Gilbert Gutiérrez C.
Ramo: Any Lynne Peggs y Anthony Roller
Rosario: Cecilia García M. y M. Ricardo Rodríguez H.
Libro: Norma Mercharie S. y César García M.
Arras: Anitelise y Francisco Núñez
Cojines: Monique Be. y Francis Bastiffka

Flores

Martin Rodríguez Ch. y Eduardo García M.
Tania Rodríguez C. y Joseph Rodríguez A.

Figure 1   Wedding invitations.

pearance of parents' names seems to be the unmarked, or more conventional, form. The text in Spanish (from the United States–Mexican border) also includes names of those participating in the ceremony: the people who have been chosen to provide the various elements (the rope, the "book," etc.) that are essential to weddings in this culture. Thus, although there are usually repeated elements that are carried from text to text in this and other genres, every situated text is a negotiated revision, modified by the social forces in its particular context.

The obituary

Another easily recognizable "homely" genre is the obituary, a category that is well known to newspaper readers throughout the world. If we think about obituaries only in terms of our own cultures, we might assume that texts from these genres are very similar in content, form, and purpose. However, after completing studies of obituaries from a variety of locations throughout the United States, Fielden (1995) found that there can be considerable variation even within one country, particularly in terms of content. In small towns, for example, much of the text is devoted to blood lines and relationships: Generations of ancestors are mentioned, as are all of those in the family who survived the deceased. In larger cities, the focus is more on the profession and accomplishments of the deceased and the contributions he or she made to the community. In both cases, the cause of death is usually mentioned, and readers are advised about which charity is accepting donations in memory of the deceased. Obituaries from other parts of the world may have different purposes and content.

Pena (1995) studied the obituary pages from several Brazilian newspapers, a few of which are translated from the Portuguese in Figure 2. She found that these texts are generally devoted either to anniversary masses (#1 and #6 in Figure 2) or to expressions of thanks to individuals who were helpful during the deceased's final illness (#7). This researcher found no death announcements in Brazilian newspapers, no information about cause or time of death, or about where contributions might be made in memory of the deceased.

Kishida (1995) studied Japanese obituary pages from the three major national newspapers, discovering two types of texts: the longer biographical article for important individuals and the shorter version, "Death and Funeral Notices." She discovered remarkable similarities in content and moves among the shorter "Death and Funeral" texts, which will be discussed here.

As can be seen from Figure 3, the name of the deceased is listed first in *kanji* (Chinese script), then it is written in *hiragana* or *katakana*, other

1 ENGINEER BRUNO PEREIRA DE LYRA
(1 YEAR ANNIVERSARY)

Elide Philippini Pereira de Lyra invite the relatives and friends to the First Year Mass of the death of the unforgetable son BRUNO on 12/28/94 (Wed.) at 8 a.m. at the Church of the Immaculate Conception
904 Gavea Road - 266 Botafogo Beach

❖❖❖

3 LUIZ FEIJO

Third chair senior professor of Clinical Medicine - UFRJ (Federal University of Rio de Janeiro). I ask God to protect him and I am thankful for knowing him.

Isabella Feijo

❖❖❖

5 ESTERLINA DE PAIVA CAVALCANTI
(Mass of the 7th Day)

Nelma, Sylvio and Joao Paulo Pedroza, daughter, son-in-law, and grandson, thank you for the feelings of sorrow received at the funeral and invite you to the Mass of the 7th Day which will be held December 26, 1994, Monday, at 10:30 a.m., Sao Conrado Church, 904 Gavea Road - Sao Conrado.

6 PROFESSORA NELY TEIXEIRA GONCALVES

The students, employees, management, and professional colleagues of the MVI Teaching Network invite you to the Mass of the 7th Day of the dear and sweet friend, Nely Teixeira Goncalves, 12/29, Monday, at 9:00 a.m., at the Church of Sao Jose and Our Lady of Conception - A maro Cavalcante Ave. (Engenheiro de Dentro)

❖❖❖

7 THANKS

At the moment that we were hit by deep pain with the overwhelming loss of our dear Aurinha we have received kindness, support, and solidarity from the people at the Hotel Brazil of Sao Lourenco, especially Mr. Charlo Lage and Mr. Toninho. Equally, we state our sincere thanks to the doctors, nurses, and aides of the intensive care unit of the first wing - with special reference to Drs. Samuel Goncalves de Moraes and Tarcisio Vieira de Carvalho, resident Bernardo and nurse Edna - and everyone from the Hospital Foundation "Casa de Caridade Sao Lourenco," who was persistent in the assistance that was given to us and our family.

Maria and Aracy Dias de Araujo

Figure 2   Translations of Brazilian obituaries. (Pena, 1995)

Japanese scripts, so that readers will know how to pronounce it.[2] The cause of death and the exact time and date are then listed, followed by the age of the deceased. The time and place of the funeral service and the name of the chief mourner (generally the wife or eldest son) are also included, along with the home address of the family.

Kishida explains these repeated features in terms of the norms of her culture. The name of the deceased is presented in *kanji* because this is the most formal Japanese script. However, the *kanji* must be translated into *hiragana* or *katakana* because readers need to have the correct pronunciation, something the *kanji* alone cannot provide. Kishida notes that there are at least two reasons for reporting the exact time of death: the readers' expectations for this convention ("their right to know") and the fact that time, like weather, is important to Japanese literary genres, especially *haiku* and *tanka* poetry. The name of the chief mourner is central to the understanding of Japanese funeral practices. This person is the ceremonial family representative, who expresses appreciation to those who attend the memorial service and send condolences. Finally, there is the family's home address, listed so that those who read the obituary will know where to send letters, telegrams, and gifts. In many Japanese companies, someone is assigned to read the obituaries and to send appropriate condolences to business associates or politicians; thus, this final content element serves several purposes.

What can we say about obituaries as a genre? What conventions are repeated and shared across cultures? Very few, beyond the name of the deceased. Even the purposes are clouded. Though most obituaries announce the death itself, others, such as those in Brazil, announce the funeral masses. Thus, obituary genre schemata for newspaper readers will vary considerably depending on the cultural context. On the other hand, the shared name for the genre and the general sense of purpose and reading context (typically, in a special section in newspapers) provide for us a history, an avenue for recognizing and processing obituaries within, as well as outside, our own cultural and linguistic contexts.

Using "homely" genres to begin a discussion of social construction of texts can remind students of the broad genre knowledge they already possess. They know, often implicitly, that many forces influence texts, including the readers' and writer's genre knowledge, the culture of the country or community, the language, a nation's literary history, and the purposes of individual readers and writers. Studying known texts helps students to remember that no text can be considered autonomous or free from the various social and cultural factors that contribute to its production.

2 As speakers of Chinese know, characters can be variously pronounced depending on the dialect (Mandarin, Cantonese, etc.).

From the *Yomiuri*, Apr. 5 1995

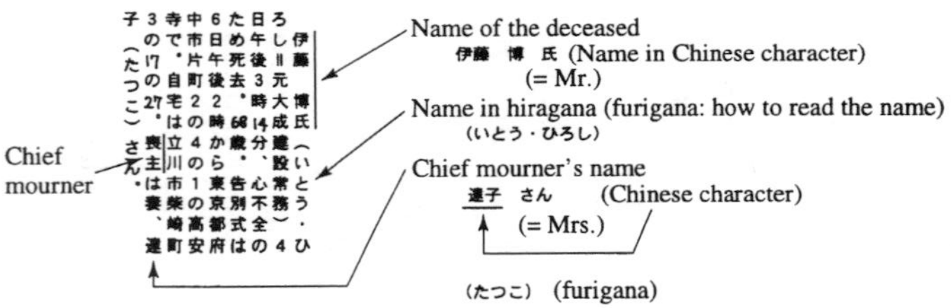

チ3神4た日ろ
のて帯自かの午し伊
たけ片野発午し伊
二2 での時2。時大博
二は純成氏
去親立の4か殿分ろ
。主川1東告殿不ろい
は市の東の葬不答と
書葬の府の死別不ろ
運安府は死ひ

→ Name of the deceased
伊藤 博 氏 (Name in Chinese character)
(= Mr.)
→ Name in hiragana (furigana: how to read the name)
(いとう・ひろし)

Chief
mourner
→ Chief mourner's name
道子 さん (Chinese character)
(= Mrs.)

(たつこ) (furigana)

From the *Asahi*, Apr 5 1995

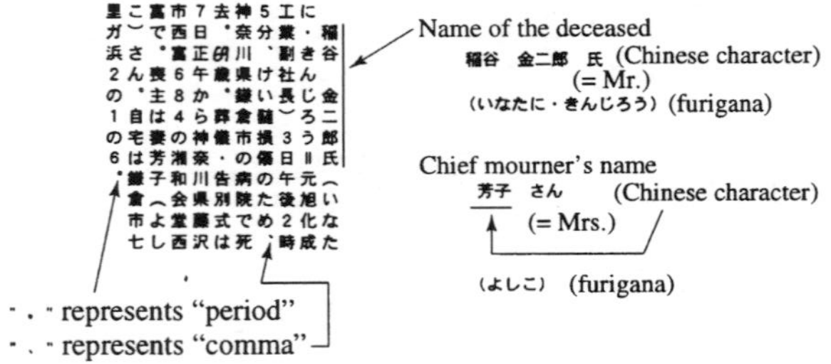

星に市7主神5工に
ガして西日・葬分葉・開
兵え蓬正研川・町者ぬ
2ん奥6午葉県け社ん
の・主8か・難い氏じ金
1目は4ら葬葉継う5二
の宅葉の神横市須35郎
6は葉横市須日Ⅲ氏
・葬子和川告葬の午元い
・全県葬別た企追い
市よ主葉式であ2化な
セし西葉式で死時成た

→ Name of the deceased
昭和 金二郎 氏 (Chinese character)
(= Mr.)
(いわたに・きんじろう) (furigana)

→ Chief mourner's name
芳子 さん (Chinese character)
(= Mrs.)

(よしこ) (furigana)

"。" represents "period"
"、" represents "comma"

[name in furigana]   [occupation]
(Ito Saburo=moto Hitachi Zosen jo:mu, moto Tsu:sansho: keiko:gyo: kyokucho.
(Ito Saburo=moto Hitachi Zosen jo:mu, moto Tsu:sansho: keiko:gyo: kyokucho.

[date and time of death]   [cause of death]
muyuka gogo kuji sanju-pun, haien no tame,
muyuka gogo kuji sanju-pun, kaien no tame

[place of death]   [age at death]
Toykyo-to Shinjuku-ku no byo:in de, shikyo. Nanaju:hachi sai.
                                          shikyo. Nanaju:hachi sai.

[date and time of funeral service]
So:gi kokubetsu-shiki wa to:ka sho:go kara
Kokubetsu-shiki wa to:ka sho:go kara

[place of funeral service]
Minato-ku Shibako:en yon-no-nana-no-sanju:go no Zo:jo:ji de.
Tokyo-to Minato-ku Shibako:en yon-no-nana-no-sanju:go no Zo:jo:ji de.

[name of chief mourner]
Moshu wa tsuma Setsuko-san.
Moshu wa tsuma Setsuko-san.

[home address]
Jitaku wa Yokohama-shi tsurumi-ku higashi-terao nakadai ju:ni-no-ju:hachi.
Jitaku wa Yokohama-shi tsurumi-ku higashi-terao nakadai ju:ni-no-ju:hachi.

The translation based upon the Asahi version:
Mr. Saburo Ito
(previous executive of Hitachi Zo:sen Inc., previous engineering chief of MIT*)
*Ministry of International Trade and Industry
(He) died of pneumonia at a hospital in Shinjuku, tokyo, at 9:30 p.m., the sixth. (He was) 78 years old. The funeral service, funeral ceremony (will be) at Zo:jo: temple: 4-7-35, Shiba Park, Minato-ku, at noon, the 10th. The chief mourner (is, his) wife, Setsuko. (His) home address (is) 12-18, Nakadai, Higashi-terao, Tsurumi-ku, Yokohama-shi.

The following shows the seven elements of the obituary about the same person in two newspapers, the *Asahi and Yomiuri*, arranged in parallel construction.

1. From the *Asahi*, Mar. 8 1995
2. From the *Yomiuri*, Mar. 8 1995

[name]
Ito Saburo shi
Ito Saburo shi

Figure 3 Japanese obituaries. (Kishida, 1995)

Neither we nor our students can establish with complete confidence the particular generic conventions that will always be repeated, nor can we predict how texts within a genre will evolve. However, we can encourage students to carry their genre knowledge from one context to another and to assess a current textual experience in light of analogous past situations. As they proceed, they must always keep in mind these cautions: "[that a text] provides clues to its own meaning, so when we anticipate a text's genre, we begin to know how to interpret it. [We say] *begin to know* because a genre never remains fixed" (Kent, 1993, p. 127). Thus, through analyzing familiar, "homely" texts and revising their genre schemata for various contexts, students can develop methods for examining academic and professional discourses with increasing sophistication.

Faculty genres

Some of the most extensive and interesting work on the social construction of texts relates to the professional genres of academic faculty, particularly the research article (see especially Bhatia, 1993, and Swales, 1990). The studies of these and other genres have revealed what has been discussed in this and the previous chapters: that the production of texts is highly complex, no matter how formalized and predictable the final versions may appear to be. Thus, although research articles in some scientific journals may appear to the uninitiated to be somewhat stable in terms of form and argumentation, considerable dialogue, and often conflict, within laboratories, on e-mail, and elsewhere often takes place before the published version is written. Even within the published texts, there are signs of conflict, or alternatively, of solidarity within a community. For example, Myers (1989) found that scientists use various types of politeness strategies, such as hedging, to demonstrate their solidarity with readers of their texts.

Some genres do not appear, even at first glance, to be stable across texts. In literature, and in other humanities disciplines, unstable and unpredictable texts are often valued: Readers appreciate texts for variability in style and the complexity of narrative. Thus, Clifford (1986, p. 5) refers to good literature as "inherently unstable . . . playing upon the stratification of meaning." Because of the textual values in literature, faculty from this discipline may find the seemingly predictable texts of science and engineering to be dull, unimaginative, or poorly written (see Spack, 1988). On the other hand, scientists and engineers sometimes criticize writing in literature as "mere word play." They say, "This work is not rigorous."

These differences between texts and the values that support them can spill over into academic classrooms, affecting students who may be familiar with the genres in one discipline but enrolled in classes of another. Students can thus become confused and unable to adjust to the implicit discourse rules of various disciplines. They are seldom told about textual conventions, principally because the rules have become second nature to their instructors, who have already been initiated into disciplinary practices.

Pedagogical genres

Many of our students do not read or write texts from the professional genres of a discipline until they are quite advanced. Instead, they are assigned to read pedagogical genres, generally textbooks,[3] that are developed primarily to introduce students to a discipline. When novice students write, they are asked to produce discourses in some of the pedagogical genres mentioned earlier: the essay examination response, the term paper, or the pedagogical summary (see Horowitz, 1986a).

The textbook

Reading is more common than writing in many academic classes (Johns, 1981b),[4] particularly at the undergraduate level, so this discussion will focus on pedagogical genres with reading demands, especially from textbooks. In many classrooms the textbook is the chief reading source, the single window into the values and practices of a discipline. This is particularly the case in science and technology. Thomas Kuhn noted the following about the importance of textbooks in the sciences:

Perhaps the most striking feature of scientific education is that, to an extent quite unknown in other creative fields, it is conducted through textbooks, works written especially for students. Until he is ready, or very nearly ready, to begin his dissertation, the student of chemistry, physics, astronomy, geology, or biology is seldom asked to attempt trial research projects or exposed to the immediate products of research done by others – to, that is, the professional communications that scientists write for their peers (1963, p. 362).

Thus, in some disciplines, it is textbooks that initially shape their views. Myers (1992) and Kuhn (1963) argue that there are considerable disadvantages to the use of volumes from this single genre as the primary sources of knowledge, methodology, and argumentation, especially in the

3 The assigned volumes for courses are sometimes called "coursebooks"; however, I will be referring to them as textbooks.
4 Though my 1981 study was conducted in a comprehensive university in the United States, it has been replicated in several other countries, including Saudi Arabia. The findings were similar: Reading and listening are the most important academic skills except in advanced graduate classes.

sciences, where research moves ahead with considerable speed. Myers (1992, p. 5) notes that in textbooks, students are presented with a "body of knowledge backed by [disciplinary] consensus." By the time this information appears in textbooks, having migrated through laboratories and professional genres for several years, it is old information to academic professionals. The scientists have gone on to other topics, methods, and argumentation. Thus, what students read is outdated material.

Critics of scientific textbooks also complain that these volumes fail to portray the complex life of a group of scientists attempting to break the knowledge and methodology barriers. Textbooks fail to discuss the conflicts among scientists or the politics of the scientific communities. They also fail to indicate the tentative nature of scientific conclusions, hedged with phrases such as "perhaps" and "might suggest" in research articles. Like most encyclopedia articles and undergraduate lectures, textbooks tend to depict science as "facts," not as methodologically complex and provisional, contradictory and constantly evolving. The grammar of textbooks underscores this factual orientation: Assertions about the "facts" of science are generally unmodified. The present tense is employed ("*A* has a certain relation to *B*"), giving students the impression that they are being told universal truths (Latour & Woolgar, 1986, p. 77). Though nonlinear features, such as graphs and formulas, are included in textbooks, they frequently illustrate a point rather than serve purposes integral to argumentation, as is the case in most scientific research articles (Myers, 1992).

Other features also distinguish textbooks from professional academic genres. Crismore (1985), drawing from work on "considerate text" (see Armbruster & Anderson, 1984), completed a survey of the metadiscourse, or discourse about discourse (see Chapter 7), of nine social studies textbooks designed at a number of academic levels (for students ages 10 to 20), comparing these volumes to discourses from professional academic genres. She found, among other things, that there was considerably more evidence of authors' attitudes toward the topics discussed in the professional writing as shown by the metadiscoursal comments ("obviously," "we must note that"). On the other hand, readers of textbooks hardly know that the writers are there, for writers' views and purposes are seldom displayed in metadiscoursal features. Most of these analyses of textbooks have been completed in the sciences; however, many of the same claims can be made for textbooks in other disciplines as well.

One problematic result of the exclusive classroom use of textbooks is that students become conditioned to believe that all written discourses are "autonomous and context free repositories of factual information" (Haas, 1994, p. 43); " . . . students [thus] may hold an atheoretical or asituational theory of written discourse, a representation or model of discourse that precludes seeing text as motivated activity and authors as purposeful agents" (p. 46).

Despite (or perhaps because of) these weaknesses, textbooks are not going to be discarded in academic classrooms. Faculty find them to be useful in providing an organized view of the discipline and disciplinary consensus, and they exploit many of the textbook aids, such as summaries and study questions, in their teaching. In literacy classes, however, we can challenge the students' theories of these and other genres as "autonomous and context free repositories of factual information" (Haas, 1994, p. 43). With the assistance of our faculty colleagues in other disciplines, we can help students to understand that, like all genres, textbooks are motivated by a variety of forces. We can begin, for example, with the complex consideration of primary readership, or audience (see Swales, 1995), asking "For whom are textbooks written?" Initially, it might be argued that the students are the primary readership, for

Publishers (and the authors) devote considerable energy to providing an attractive cover and layout and to making the material "transparent" to students (Swales, 1995, p. 6).

But are the students the primary audiences? Do they select the textbooks for use? Alred and Thelen (1993, p. 469) note that "both publishers and authors are well aware that while the . . . textbook is addressed to the student audience, the textbook is constructed for a professional audience." Swales notes that

. . . it is we professionals who evaluate manuscripts, write reviews, peruse catalogues, visit book exhibits, recommend adoptions and orchestrate the use of textbooks in classes. It is not the students who do these things, however much we may value the *different* kind of feedback students may provide. Textbook authoring is thus – and despite appearance to the contrary – more dialogic (cf. Bakhtin 1986) with the evaluator-reader than with the consumer-reader (Swales, 1995, p. 6).

Armed with this knowledge, students can explore with us, or with other faculty, motivations for text selection, and thus begin to understand some community or classroom goals and values. Over the past few years, my students and I have been interviewing discipline-specific (DS) faculty about their selections of textbooks, an exercise that is revealing for both the interviewers and those interviewed. Faculty tell us that there are several reasons for their choices: the textbook covers the necessary course content with the appropriate balance among topics; it includes "helps" for students such as chapter summaries, illustrations, problems, computer aids, and comprehension questions; it is readable for a particular student population; or, in some cases, the faculty member is the author and has written the textbook for the class.

In addition to interviewing instructors about what motivates their choices, we, and our students, can work with faculty to compare textbook renditions of the "same" information. An economics professor who visited one of our literacy classes brought three introductory economics textbooks for student consideration. He consulted the three explanations of the "circular flow," a chart and text demonstrating how money circulates in a capitalist society. To his surprise, he discovered that the presentations of this "accepted" theory in the three textbooks were considerably different, in terms of how the concept was introduced through written text, the visual explanation, and the examples. He and the students decided that they could be led to understand the "circular flow" in considerably different ways, depending on the textbook selected. This discovery enabled all parties involved to come to terms with textbook variation even in the presentation of "consensual information."

We can also work with students and DS faculty to analyze selected elements within student textbooks and discuss the purposes they serve. For example, examining and discussing the purposes of visuals as they interact with texts assists students to recognize these nonlinear elements as integral to textbook genres. Students can divide into groups, each assigned to a visual element in their textbooks. Each group then studies how the written and nonlinear texts interact and evaluates the usefulness of the visual in promoting their understanding of a concept or process. The groups then report and discuss their findings. Textbook language can also be studied as motivated and genre-based. Students can test Myers's (1992) claims that information is presented as "fact" through the use of present tense and the absence of hedging. They can compare the textbook language at a number of levels (grammatical, lexical, cohesive) with the language found in examples of other genres in the discipline, such as research articles. Students can also examine textbook organization. They can ask themselves, or a faculty informant, "Why are chapters organized in this way? What did the authors intend for us to understand when they developed this organization? What topics are discussed in the major chapter sections? Why? What does this indicate about these authors' understanding of the discipline or disciplinary consensus?" In using activities of this type, we begin to break down students' theories of autonomous, unmotivated texts and to assist them in understanding that all written discourses draw from other texts, are written for one or more audiences, and are prepared and selected by individuals with particular backgrounds and interests.

This chapter has continued the discussion of genre, arguing that this concept is an abstraction shared by readers and writers with similar textual experiences. Some "homely" genres have been presented, and a few of the issues relating to professional academic genres have been explored. I have suggested ways in which a textbook can be an object of research and inquiry, of interest to both students and discipline-specific faculty. Though there is much more that we need to understand about genres and the relationship of this concept to particular texts, roles and contexts, it still presents rich possibilities for exploitation in the development of academic literacies and in understanding what motivates texts.

4 *Discourse communities and communities of practice*

Membership, conflict, and diversity

If there is one thing that most of [the discourse community definitions] have in common, it is an idea of language [and genres] as a basis for sharing and holding in common: shared expectations, shared participation, commonly (or communicably) held ways of expressing. Like audience, discourse community entails assumptions about conformity and convention (Rafoth, 1990, p. 140).

What is needed for descriptive adequacy may not be so much a search for the conventions of language use in a particular group, but a search for the varieties of language use that work both with and against conformity, and accurately reflect the interplay of identity and power relationships (Rafoth, 1990, p. 144).

A second important concept in the discussion of socioliteracies is *discourse community*. Because this term is abstract, complex, and contested,[1] I will approach it by attempting to answer a few of the questions that are raised in the literature, those that seem most appropriate to teaching and learning in academic contexts.

1. Why do individuals join social and professional communities? What appear to be the relationships between communities and their genres?
2. Are there levels of community? In particular, can we hypothesize a "general academic community" or language?
3. What are some of the forces that make communities complex and varied? What forces work against "shared participation and shared ways of expressing?" (Rafoth, 1990, p. 140).

I have used the term discourse communities because this appears to be the most common term in the literature. However, *communities of practice*, a related concept, is becoming increasingly popular, particularly for academic contexts (see Brown & Duguid, 1995; Lave & Wenger, 1991). In the term *discourse communities*, the focus is on texts and language, the genres and lexis that enable members throughout the world to maintain their goals, regulate their membership, and communicate efficiently with

1 Some of the contested issues and questions are: "How are communities defined?" (Rafoth, 1990); "Do discourse communities even exist?" (Prior, 1994); "Are they global or local? Or both?" (Killingsworth, 1992); "What is the relationship between discourse communities and genres?" (Swales, 1988b, 1990).

one another. Swales (1990, pp. 24–27) lists six defining characteristics of a discourse community:

1. [It has] a broadly agreed set of common public goals.
2. [It has] mechanisms of intercommunication among its members (such as newsletters or journals).
3. [It] utilizes and hence possesses one or more genres in the communicative furtherance of its aims.
4. [It] uses its participatory mechanisms primarily to provide information and feedback.
5. In addition to owning genres, [it] has acquired some specific lexis.
6. [It has] a threshold level of members with a suitable degree of relevant content and discoursal expertise.

The term communities of practice refers to genres and lexis, but especially to many practices and values that hold communities together or separate them from one another. Lave and Wenger, in discussing students' enculturation into academic communities, have this to say about communities of practice:

As students begin to engage with the discipline, as they move from exposure to experience, they begin to understand that the different communities on campus are quite distinct, that apparently common terms have different meanings, apparently shared tools have different uses, apparently related objects have different interpretations. . . . As they work in a particular community, they start to understand both its particularities and what joining takes, how these involve language, practice, culture and a conceptual universe, not just mountains of facts (1991, p. 13).

Thus, communities of practice are seen as complex collections of individuals who share genres, language, values, concepts, and "ways of being" (Geertz, 1983), often distinct from those held by other communities.

In order to introduce students to these visions of community, it is useful to take them outside the academic realm to something more familiar, the recreational and avocational communities to which they, or their families, belong. Thus I begin with a discussion of nonacademic communities before proceeding to issues of academic communities and membership.

Communities and membership

Social, political, and recreational communities

People are born, or taken involuntarily by their families and cultures, into some communities of practice. These first culture communities may be religious, tribal, social, or economic, and they may be central to an individual's daily life experiences. Academic communities, on the other hand, are selected and voluntary, at least after compulsory education. There-fore, this chapter will concentrate on communities that are chosen, the groups with which people maintain ties because of their interests, their politics, or their professions. Individuals are often members of a variety of communities outside academic life: social and interest groups with which they have chosen to affiliate. These community affiliations vary in terms of individual depth of interest, belief, and commitment. Individual in-volvement may become stronger or weaker over time as circumstances and interests change.

Nonacademic communities of interest, like "homely" genres, can pro-vide a useful starting point for student discussion. In presenting com-munities of this type, Swales uses the example of the Hong Kong Study Circle (HKSC),[2] of which he is a paying member, whose purposes are to "foster interest in and knowledge of the stamps of Hong Kong" (1990, p. 27). He was once quite active in this community, dialoging frequently with other members through HKSC publications.[3] However, at this point in his life, he has other interests (birds and butterflies), and so he is now an inactive member of HKSC. His commitments of time and energy have been diverted elsewhere.

Members of my family are also affiliated with several types of com-munities. We are members of cultural organizations, such as the local art museum and the theater companies. We receive these communities' pub-lications, and we attend some of their functions, but we do not consider ourselves to be active. We also belong to a variety of communities with political aims. My mother, for example, is a member of the powerful lobbying group, the American Association of Retired Persons (AARP). The several million members pay their dues because of their interests in maintaining government-sponsored retirement (Social Security) and health benefits (Medicare), both of which are promoted by AARP lobby-ists in the U.S. Congress. The AARP magazine, *Modern Maturity*, is a powerful organ of the association, carefully crafted to forward the group's aims. Through this publication, members are urged to write to their elected representatives about legislation, and they are also informed about which members of Congress are "friends of the retired." However, members are offered more than politics: Articles in the magazine discuss keeping healthy while aging, remaining beautiful, traveling cheaply, and using the Internet. AARP members also receive discounts on prescription drugs, tours, and other benefits.[4]

2 Note that most communities use abbreviations for their names and often for their publications. All community members recognize these abbreviations, of course.
3 These written interactions are impossible for the noninitiated to understand, I might point out.
4 When I asked my mother to drop her AARP membership because of a political stand

Recently, my husband has become very active in a recreational discourse community, the international community of cyclists.[5] He reads publications such as *Bicycling* ("World's No. 1 Road and Mountain Bike Magazine") each month for advice about better cyclist health ("Instead of Pasta, Eat This!"),[6] equipment to buy, and international cycling tours. Like most other communities, cycling has experts, some of whom write articles for the magazines to which he subscribes, using a register that is mysterious to the uninitiated: "unified gear triangle"; "metal matrix composite." Cyclists share values (good health, travel interests), special knowledge, vocabulary, and genres, but they do not necessarily share political or social views, as my husband discovered when conversing with other cyclists on a group trip. In publications for cyclists, we can find genres that we recognize by name but with community-related content: editorials, letters to the editor, short articles on new products, articles of interest to readers (on health and safety, for example), advertisements appealing to readers, and essay/commentaries. If we examine magazines published for other interest groups, we can find texts from many of the same genres.

As this discussion indicates, individuals often affiliate with several communities at the same time, with varying levels of involvement and interest. People may join a group because they agree politically, because they want to socialize, or because they are interested in a particular sport or pastime. The depth of an individual's commitment can, and often does, change over time. As members come and go, the genres and practices continue to evolve, reflecting and promoting the active members' aims, interests, and controversies.

Studying the genres of nonacademic communities, particularly those with which students are familiar, helps them to grasp the complexity of text production and processing and the importance of understanding the group practices, lexis, values, and controversies that influence the construction of texts.

Professional communities

Discourse communities can also be professional; every major profession has its organizations, its practices, its textual conventions, and its genres. Active community members also carry on informal exchanges: at conferences, through e-mail interest groups, in memos, in hallway discus-

---

the organization took, she said, "I can't, Ann. I get too good a deal on my medicines through my membership."

5 Those of us who are outsiders call them "gearheads." Often, terms are applied to insiders by community outsiders.

6 Brill, D. (1994, November). What's free of fat and cholesterol, costs 4 cents per serving, and has more carbo than pasta? Rice! *Bicycling*, pp. 86–87.

sions at the office, in laboratories and elsewhere, the results of which may be woven intertextually into public, published texts. However, it is the written genres of communities that are accessible to outsiders for analysis. We need only to ask professionals about their texts in order to collect an array of interesting examples. One of the most thoroughly studied professional communities is the law. In his *Analysing Genre: Language Use in Professional Settings* (1993), Bhatia discusses at some length his continuing research into legal communities that use English and other languages (pp. 101–143). He identifies the various genres of the legal profession: their purposes, contexts, and the form and content that appear to be conventional. He also contrasts these genres as they are realized in texts from various cultures.

However, there are many other professional discourse communities whose genres can be investigated, particularly when students are interested in enculturation. For example, students might study musicians who devote their lives to pursuing their art but who also use written texts to dialogue with others in their profession. To learn more about these communities, I interviewed a bassoonist in our city orchestra.[7] Along with those who play oboe, English horn, and contrabassoon, this musician subscribes to the major publication of the double-reed community, *The International Double Reed Society Journal*. Though he has specialized, double-reed interests, he reports that he and many other musicians also have general professional aims and values that link them to musicians in a much broader community. He argues that all practicing musicians within the Western tradition[8] share knowledge; there is a common core of language and values within this larger community. Whether they are guitarists, pianists, rock musicians, or bassoonists, musicians in the West seem to agree, for example, that the strongest and most basic musical intervals are 5–1 and 4–1, and that other chord intervals are weaker. They share a basic linguistic register and an understanding of chords and notation. Without this sharing, considerable negotiation would have to take place before they could play music together. As in other professions, these musicians have a base of expertise, values, and expectations that they use to facilitate communication. Thus, though a musician's first allegiance may be to his or her own musical tradition (jazz) or instrument (the bassoon), he or she will still share a great deal with other expert musicians – and much of this sharing is accomplished through specialized texts.

What can we conclude from this section about individual affiliations

---

7 I would like to thank Arlan Fast of the San Diego Symphony for these community insights.

8 Knowledge is also shared with musicians from other parts of the world, of course. However, some of the specific examples used here apply to the Western musical tradition.

with discourse communities? First, many people have chosen to be members of one or a variety of communities, groups with whom they share social, political, professional, or recreational interests. These communities use written discourses that enable members to keep in touch with each other, carry on discussions, explore controversies, and advance their aims; the genres are their vehicles for communication. These genres are not, in all cases, sophisticated or intellectual, literary or high-browed. They are, instead, representative of the values, needs, and practices of the community that produces them. Community membership may be concentrated or diluted; it may be central to a person's life or peripheral. Important for the discussion that follows is the juxtaposition of generalized and specialized languages and practices among these groups. Musicians, lawyers, athletes, and physicians, for example, may share certain values, language, and texts with others within their larger community, though their first allegiance is to their specializations. Figure 1 illustrates this general/specific relationship in communities.

In the case of physicians, for example, there is a general community and a set of values and concepts with which most may identify because they have all had a shared basic education before beginning their specializations. There are publications, documents, concepts, language, and values that all physicians can, and often do, share. The same can be said of academics, as is shown in the figure. There may be some general academic discourses,[9] language, values, and concepts that most academics share. Thus faculty often identify themselves with a college or university and its language and values, as well as with the more specialized areas of interest for which they have been prepared.

This broad academic identification presents major problems for scholars and literacy practitioners, for although it is argued that disciplines are different (see Bartholomae, 1985; Belcher & Braine, 1995; Berkenkotter & Huckin, 1995; Carson et al., 1992; Lave & Wenger, 1991, among others), many faculty believe that there is a general academic English as well as a general set of critical thinking skills and strategies for approaching texts.

Because this belief in a general, shared academic language is strong and universal, the next section of this chapter is devoted to this topic.

Academic communities

What motivates this section more than anything else is its usefulness as a starting point in the exploration of academic literacies and its accessibil-

---

9 For example, *The Chronicle of Higher Education* and several pedagogical publications are directed to a general academic audience.

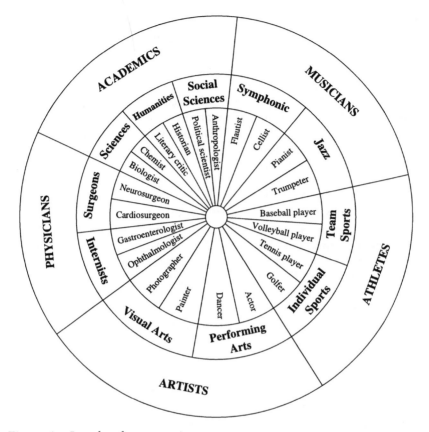

Figure 1   Levels of community.

ity to students at various levels of instruction who need to become more aware of the interaction of roles, texts, and contexts in academic communities. Many literacy faculty have mixed classes of students from a number of disciplines or students just beginning to consider what it means to be an academic reader and writer. For these students, and even for some of the more advanced, a discussion of what are considered to be general academic languages and textual practices is a good place to start their analyses – although not a good place to finish.

In the previous section it was noted that professionals may affiliate at various levels of specificity within their discourse communities. They often share language, knowledge, and values with a large, fairly heterogeneous group, though their first allegiances may be with a specialized group within this broader "club." This comment can apply to individuals in academic communities as well. Faculty have their own discipline-specific allegiances (to biology, chemistry, sociology, engineering); nonetheless, many believe that there are basic, generalizable linguistic, textual, and rhetorical rules for the entire academic community that can apply.

Discipline-specific faculty who teach novices at the undergraduate level, and some who teach graduate students as well, sometimes complain that their students "do not write like academics" or "cannot comprehend" academic prose, arguing that these are general abilities that we should be teaching. The discussion that follows acknowledges their complaints and sets the stage for discussions of more specific academic issues and pedagogies in later chapters.

LANGUAGE, TEXTS, AND VALUES

This section on academic textual practices draws principally from three sources: "Reflections on Academic Discourse" (Elbow, 1991); *Words and Lives: The Anthropologist as Author* (Geertz, 1988); and *The Scribal Society: An Essay on Literacy and Schooling in the Information Age* (Purves, 1990) (see also Dudley-Evans, 1995). Elbow and Purves are well-known composition theorists from different theoretical camps who were cited in Chapter 1. Geertz, an anthropologist, has studied academic communities and their genres for many years. All three of these experts live in the United States, and this may affect their views; however, in many universities in the world in which English is employed, these beliefs about general text features are also shared, except perhaps in literature and some of the humanities disciplines. Following is a composite of the arguments made by the three academics about the nature, values, and practices in general expository academic prose, including some commentary on each topic.

1. *Texts must be explicit.* Writers should select their vocabulary carefully and use it wisely. In some cases, such as with certain noun compounds, paraphrase is impossible because specialized academic vocabulary must be used. Citation must be constructed carefully. Data analysis should be described and discussed explicitly. The methodology should be stated so clearly that it is replicable. Ambiguity in argumentation should be avoided.

Comment. Faculty often complain that students are "careless" in their use of vocabulary, in their citation practices, and in their argumentation and use of data. Because many literacy classes value the personal essay and because many readings in literacy classes are in story form or are adapted or specially written for these classes, students are not exposed to the exactness of some academic prose. One of our responsibilities in developing socioliterate practices is to expose students to authentic academic texts and to analyze these texts for their specificity.

2. *Topic and argument should be prerevealed in the introduction.* Purves says that experienced academics, particularly when writing certain

kinds of texts, should "select a single aspect of [a] subject and announce [their] theses and purposes as soon as possible" (1990, p. 12).

Comment. Finding the argument in a reading and noticing how data, examples, or narration are used to support this argument are essential academic abilities that are praised by faculty from many disciplines. In like manner, understanding and presenting a clear argument that is appropriate to a genre are writing skills that appear high on faculty wish lists for students, particularly for those who come from diverse rhetorical traditions (see Connor, 1987). Most faculty require that arguments and purposes appear early, generally in an introduction. One of the discipline-specific faculty with whom I work tells her students not to "spend much time clearing their throats." She wants them to "get right down to the argument."

We must be aware, however, that the pressure to reveal topic, purposes, and argumentation early in a written text may be a culture-specific value and apply only to certain kinds of texts within specific communities. There is considerable discussion in the contrastive rhetoric and World Englishes literature about the motivations for text organization and content and the necessity (or lack thereof) for prerevealing information. Local cultures and first languages, as well as academic disciplines, can influence how and where arguments appear.

3. *Writers should provide "maps" or "signposts" for the readers throughout the texts, telling the readers where they have been in the text and where they are going.* By using a variety of tactics, writers can assist readers in predicting and summarizing texts and in understanding the relationships among topics and arguments. Most of these tactics fall under the metadiscourse rubric.

Comment. Metadiscourse is defined in the following way:

> It is writing about reading and writing. When we communicate, we use metadiscourse to name rhetorical actions: *explain, show, argue, claim, deny, suggest, add, expand, summarize;* to name the part of our discourse, *first, second . . . in conclusion;* to reveal logical connections, *therefore . . . if so . . .* to guide our readers, *Consider the matter of* (Williams, 1989, p. 28).

Literacy textbooks for both reading and writing often emphasize the understanding and use of metadiscourse in texts. However, it is important to note that language and culture can have considerable influence on the ways in which metadiscourse is used. For example, in countries with homogeneous cultures, academic written English may have fewer metadiscoursal features (Mauranen, 1993) than in heterogeneous, "writer-responsible" cultures (see Hinds, 1987) such as the United States, Great Britain, or Australia. As in the case of all texts, academic discourses are influenced by the cultures and communities in which they are found, often in very complicated ways.

4. *The language of texts should create a distance between the writer and the text to give the appearance of objectivity.* Geertz (1988) speaks of academic, expository prose as "author-evacuated"; the author's personal voice is not clearly in evidence, because the first person pronoun is absent and arguments are muted. He compares author-evacuated prose with the "author-saturated" prose of many literary works, in which individual voice pervades. As mentioned earlier, this "author-evacuation" is particularly evident in pedagogical genres, such as the textbook. One way to create the evacuated style is to use the passive, a common rhetorical choice for the sciences, but there are other ways as well.

Comment. Discipline-specific faculty sometimes tell us that students are unable to write "objectively" or to comprehend "objective" prose.[10] These students have not mastered the ability to clothe their argumentation in a particular register, to give it the kind of objective overlay that is valued in academic circles. When I asked one of my first-year university students to tell the class what he had learned about academic English, he said: "We can't use 'I' anymore. We have to pretend that we're not there in the text." In many cases, he is right. Literacy teachers need to help students to analyze texts for their author-evacuated style, and to discuss the particular grammatical and lexical choices that are made to achieve the appearance of objectivity and distance.

5. *Texts should maintain a "rubber-gloved" quality of voice and register.* They must show a kind of reluctance to touch one's meanings with one's naked fingers (Elbow, 1991, p. 145).

Comment. For some academic contexts, writers appear to remove themselves emotionally and personally from the texts, to hold their texts at arms' length (metaphorically). The examination of texts in which this "rubber-gloved quality" is evident will provide for students some of the language to achieve these ends. What can students discover? Many academic writers abjure the use of emotional words, such as *wonderful* and *disgusting;* they hide behind syntax and "objective" academic vocabulary.

6. *Writers should take a guarded stance, especially when presenting argumentation and results.* Hedging through the use of modals (*may, might*) and other forms (*It is possible that* . . .) is perhaps the most common way to be guarded.

Comment. Hedging appears to be central to some academic discourses, particularly those that report research. In a study of two science articles on the same topic published for two different audiences, Fahenstock (1986) found that the article written for experts in the field was replete with hedges ("*appear to* hydrolyze," "*suggesting* that animal food"), as scientists carefully reported their findings to their peers. How-

---

10 "Objective" appears in quotation marks because, though academic writing may have the appearance of being objective, all texts are biased.

ever, the article written for laypersons was filled with "facts," much like those in the textbooks described in Chapter 3. For these and other reasons, we need to introduce students to expert and nonexpert texts; we need to expose them at every level to the ways in which genre, context, readers, writers, and communities affect linguistic choices.

7. *Texts should display a vision of reality shared by members of the particular discourse community to which the text is addressed (or the particular faculty member who made the assignment).*

Comment. This may be the most difficult of the general academic requirements, for views of reality are often implicit, unacknowledged by the faculty themselves and are not revealed to students. Perhaps I can show how this "reality vision" is so difficult to uncover by discussing my research on course syllabi. I have been interviewing faculty for several years about the goals for their classes, goals that are generally stated in what is called a syllabus in the United States, but might be called a class framework or schedule of assignments in other countries. These studies indicated that most faculty tend to list as goals for the course the various topics that will be studied. The focus is exclusively on content. They do not list the particular views of the world that they want students to embrace, or the understandings that they want to encourage. In a class on "Women in the Humanities," for example, the instructor listed topics to be covered in her syllabus, but she did not tell the students that she wanted them to analyze images of women in cultures in order to see how these images shape various cultural contexts. In a geography class, the instructor listed topics to be covered, but he did not tell his students about his goals for analysis and synthesis of texts. Why are the critical-thinking goals and disciplinary values hidden by most faculty? I don't know. Perhaps instructors believe that students should intuit the values, practices, and genres required in the course; or the faculty have difficulty explicitly stating goals that are not related to content. Certainly content is the most commonly discussed issue at discipline-specific (DS) curriculum meetings, and this may influence faculty choices. In a later chapter I will discuss one of the questionnaires that I use to elicit from faculty the "views of reality" or "ways of being" that my students and I would like to see stated explicitly in the syllabi.

In contrast to DS faculty, we literacy faculty are often most interested in processes and understandings, in developing students' metacognition and metalanguages – and these interests are often reflected in our syllabi. On the next page, for example, are the student goals for a first-year university writing class developed by a committee from my university's Department of Rhetoric and Writing Studies:[11]

---

11 Quandahl, E. (1995). Rhetoric and writing studies 100: A list of goals. Unpublished paper, San Diego State University, San Diego, CA.

a. To use writing to clarify and improve your understanding of issues and texts
b. To respond in writing to the thinking of others and to explore and account for your own responses
c. To read analytically and critically, making active use of what you read in your writing
d. To understand the relationships between discourse structure and the question at issue in a piece of writing, and to select appropriate structures at the sentence and discourse levels
e. To monitor your writing for the grammar and usage conventions appropriate to each writing situation
f. To use textual material as a framework for understanding and writing about other texts, data or experiences

No matter what kind of class is being taught, faculty need to discuss critical-thinking and reading and writing goals frequently with students. They need to review why students are given assignments, showing how these tasks relate to course concepts and student literacy growth.

8. *Academic texts should display a set of social and authority relations; they should show the writer's understanding of the roles they play within the text or context.*[12]

Comment. Most students have had very little practice in recognizing the language of social roles within academic contexts, although their experience with language and social roles outside the classroom is often quite rich. Some students cannot recognize when they are being talked down to in textbooks, and they cannot write in a language that shows their roles vis-à-vis the topics studied or the faculty they are addressing. These difficulties are particularly evident among ESL/EFL students; however, they are also found among many other students whose exposure to academic language has been minimal. One reason for discussing social roles as they relate to texts from a genre, whether they be "homely" discourses or professional texts, is to heighten students' awareness of the interaction of language, roles, and contexts so that they can read and write with more sophistication.

9. *Academic texts should acknowledge the complex and important nature of intertextuality, the exploitation of other texts without resorting to plagiarism.* Students need to practice reformulation and reconstruction of information so that they do not just repeat other texts by "knowl-

---

12 When I showed this point to Virginia Guleff, a graduate student, she said, "So students have to know their place!" Perhaps we should put it this way: They need to know different registers in order to play different roles. The more people use these registers, the more effective they can become and, not incidentally, the more power they can have over the situations in which they are reading or writing.

edge telling" (Bereiter & Scardamalia, 1989) but rather use these texts inventively for their purposes (called "knowledge transforming"; Bereiter & Scardamalia, 1989).

Comment. Carson (1993), in a large study of the intellectual demands on undergraduate students, found that drawing from and integrating textual sources were two of the major challenges students face in attaining academic literacy. And no wonder. Widdowson (1993, p. 27) notes that

> When people make excessive and unacknowledged use of [another's text], and are found out, we call it plagiarism. When people are astute in their stitching of textual patchwork, we call it creativity. It is not easy to tell the difference. . . . If a text is always in some degree a conglomerate of others, how independent can its meaning be?

Drawing from sources and citing them appropriately is the most obvious and most commonly discussed aspect of intertextuality. As a result, Swales and Feak (1994) claim that citation may be the defining feature of academic discourses. However, there are other, more subtle and varied borrowings from past discourses, for, as Widdowson notes, "Any particular text is produced or interpreted in reference to a previous knowledge of other texts" (1993, p. 27).

10. *Texts should comply with the genre requirements of the community or classroom.*

Comment. This, of course, is another difficult challenge for students. As mentioned earlier, pedagogical genres are often loosely named and casually described by DS faculty. It is difficult to identify the conventions of a student research paper, an essay examination response, or other pedagogical genres because, in fact, these vary considerably from class to class. Yet DS faculty expect students to understand these distinctions and to read and write appropriately for their own classes. My students and I often ask faculty: "What is a good critique for your class?" or "What is a good term paper?" We request several student-written models and, if possible, interview the faculty member about their assigned texts and tasks.

This section has outlined what may be some general rules for academic literacy, most of which are refined within each discipline and classroom. Although it would be difficult to defend several of these beliefs because of the wide range of academic discourses and practices, listing and discussing these factors can prepare students for an examination of how texts are socially constructed and whether some of the points made here are applicable to specific texts.

Of course, we also need to expose students to texts that contradict these rules for academic discourse. We should examine literary genres, which break most of the rules listed. We should look at specialized texts that have alternative requirements for register. In any of our pedagogical conversations, the objective should not be to discover truths but to explore how social and cultural forces may influence texts in various contexts.

Community conflicts and diversity

So far, the discussion of communities and their genres has focused on the uniting forces, particularly the language, practices, values, and genres that groups may share. It has been suggested that people can join communities at will and remain affiliated at levels of their own choosing. For a number of reasons, this is not entirely accurate. In some cases people are excluded from communities because they lack social standing, talent, or money, or because they live in the wrong part of town. In other cases, community membership requires a long initiatory process, and even then there is no guarantee of success. Many students work for years toward their doctoral degrees, for example, only to find that there are no faculty positions available to them or that their approach to research will not lead to advancement.

Even after individuals are fully initiated, many factors can separate them. Members of communities rebel, opposing community leaders or attempting to change the rules of the game and, by extension, the content and argumentation in the texts from shared genres. If the rebellion is successful, the rules may be changed or a new group may be formed with a different set of values and aims. There may even be a theoretical paradigm shift in the discipline. In academic communities, rebellion may result in the creation of a new unit or department, separate from the old community, as has been the case recently in my own university.[13] Even without open rebellion, there is constant dialogue and argument within communities as members thrash out their differences and juggle for power and identity, promoting their own content, argumentation, and approaches to research.

Although much could be said about factors that affect communities outside the academic realm, the following discussion will focus on a few of the rich and complex factors that give academic communities their character.

The cost of affiliation

If students want to become affiliated with academic discourse communities, or even if they want to succeed in school, they may have to

---

13 San Diego State's new Department of Rhetoric and Writing Studies is composed of composition instructors who asked to leave the Department of English, as well as of faculty from the previously independent Academic Skills Center.

make considerable sacrifices. To become active academic participants, they sometimes must make major trade-offs that can create personal and social distance between them and their families and communities. Students are asked to modify their language to fit that of the academic classroom or discipline. They often must drop, or at least diminish in importance, their affiliations to their home cultures in order to take on the values, language, and genres of their disciplinary culture. The literature is full of stories of the students who must make choices between their communities and academic lives (see, for example, Rose's *Lives on the Boundary,* 1989). In an account of his experiences, Richard Rodriquez (1982, p. 56), a child of Mexican immigrant parents, wrote the following:

What I am about to say to you has taken me more than twenty years to admit: a primary reason for my success in the classroom was that I couldn't forget that schooling was changing me and separating me from the life I had enjoyed before becoming a student. . . . If because of my schooling, I had grown culturally separated from my parents, my education has finally given me ways of speaking and caring about that fact.

Here Rodriguez is discussing his entire schooling experience; however, as students advance in schools and universities, they may be confronted with even more wrenching conflicts between their home and academic cultures and languages. In her story of a Hispanic graduate student in a Ph.D. sociology program in the United States, Casanave (1992) tells how the tension between this student's personal values and language and her chosen department's insistence on its own scientific language and genres finally drove her from her new academic community. When she could no longer explain her work in sociology in everyday language to the people of her primary communities (her family and her clients), the student decided to leave the graduate program. The faculty viewed her stance as rebellious, an open refusal to take on academic community values. By the time she left, it had become obvious to all concerned that the faculty were unable, or unwilling, to bend or to adapt some of their disciplinary rules to accommodate this student's interests, vocation, and language.

A graduate student from Japan faced other kinds of affiliation conflicts when attempting to become a successful student in a North American linguistics program (Benson, 1996). This student brought from her home university certain social expectations: about faculty roles, about her role as a student, and about what is involved in the production of texts. She believed, for example, that the faculty should provide her with models of what was expected in her papers; she felt that they should determine her research topics and hypotheses. This had been the case in her university in Japan, and she had considerable difficulty understanding why the American faculty did not conform to the practices of her home country. She tried to follow her professors' instructions with great care, but they chastised her for "lacking ideas." In her view, the faculty were being irresponsible; however, some faculty viewed her as passive, unimaginative, and dependent. What she and many other students have found is that gaining affiliation in graduate education means much more than understanding the registers of academic language.

These examples are intended to show that full involvement or affiliation in academic discourse communities requires major cultural and linguistic trade-offs from many students. Faculty expect them to accept the texts, roles, and contexts of the discipline, but acceptance requires much more sacrifice and change than the faculty may imagine. In our literacy classes, we can assist academic students in discussing the kinds of problems they encounter when attempting to resolve these conflicts. However, we can also assist our faculty colleagues, who often are unaware of their students' plight, through workshops, student presentations, and suggestions for reading.

Issues of authority

What happens after a person has become an academic initiate, after he or she has completed the degree, published, and been advanced? There are still community issues to contend with, one of which relates to authority. Bakhtin (1986, p. 88) noted that "in each epoch, in each social circle, in each small world of family, friends, acquaintances and comrades in which a human being grows and lives, there are always authoritative utterances that set the tone."

In academic circles, these "authoritative utterances" are made by journal or e-mail interest-group editors, by conference program planners, and by others. At the local level, this authority can be held by department chairs or by chairs of important committees. Prior (1994, p. 522) speaks of these academically powerful people as "an elite group that imposes its language, beliefs and values on others through control of journals, academic appointments, curricula, student examinations, research findings and so on." It is important to note that Prior extends his discussion beyond authority over colleagues to broad authority over students through curricula and examinations. This type of pedagogical authority is very important, as all students know, so it will be discussed further.

In many countries, provincial and national examinations drive the curricula, and theoretical and practical control over these examinations means authority over what students are taught. In the People's Republic of China, for example, important general English language examinations have been based for years on word frequency counts developed in several language centers throughout the country. Each "band," or proficiency level on the examination, is determined by "the most common 1,000 words," "the most common 2,000 words," and so on.[14] Although fea-

---

14 "Most common" appears in quotation marks because what is most common (other

tures of language such as grammar are tested in these examinations, it is a theory about vocabulary, based on word frequency, that is central. It is not surprising, then, that most Chinese students believe that vocabulary is *the* key to literacy, particularly the understanding of "exact" meanings of words. When I have worked with teachers in China, I have frequently been asked questions such as "What is the exact meaning of the term 'discourse'? What does 'theory' mean?" These teachers requested a single definition, something I was often unable to provide.

The centralized power over important examinations in China, over the TOEFL and graduate entrance examinations in the United States, and over the British Council Examinations in other parts of the world gives considerable authority within communities to certain test developers and examiners. This authority permits little pedagogical latitude to teachers preparing students for these "gate-keeping" examinations. As practitioners, we can use test preparation pedagogies, or we can critique these examinations (Raimes, 1990), as we should; but we cannot institute large-scale change until we gain control and authority over the examination system.

With students at all academic levels, we practitioners should raise the issues of authority, status, and control over community utterances in literacy classes. About their own social groups, we can ask: "Who has status in your clubs and why? Who has status in your ethnic or geographical communities and why? How do they exert control over people, over utterances, and over publications?" When referring to academic situations and authority, we can ask: "Who wrote this textbook? What are the authors' affiliations? Are they prestigious? How does the language of the textbook demonstrate the author's authority over the material and over the students who read the volume?" We can also ask: "Who writes your important examinations? What are their values?" Or we can ask: "Who has status in your academic classrooms? Which students have authority and why?" And finally, we might ask: "How can you gain authority in the classroom or over texts?"

Throughout a discussion of authority relationships, we need to talk about communities, language, and genres: how texts and spoken discourses are used to gain and perpetuate authority. We can assist students to analyze authoritative texts, including those of other students, and to critique authority relationships. Our students need to become

than function words) is very difficult to determine. These lists are influenced by the type of language data that is entered into the computer for the word count: whether it is written or spoken, its register, etc. If data are varied, other vocabulary become common.

At one point in my career, I attempted to develop low-proficiency English for Business textbooks for adults using a famous publisher's list of most common words. I failed because the data used to establish the frequency lists were taken from children's books. The common words in children's language and those most common in business language are considerably different (Johns, 1985).

more aware of these factors affecting their academic lives before they can hope to produce and comprehend texts that command authority within academic contexts.

Conventions and anticonventionalism

There are many other push and pull factors in academic communities, factors that create dialogue, conflict, and change. Communities evolve constantly, though established community members may attempt to maintain their power and keep the new initiates in line through control over language and genres. A student or a young faculty member can be punished for major transgressions from the norm, for attempting to move away from what the more established, initiated members expect. In order to receive a good grade (or be published), writers often must work within the rules. Understanding these rules, even if they are to be broken, appears to be essential.

As individuals within an academic community become more established and famous, they can become more anticonventional, in both their texts and their lives. Three famous rule breakers come to mind, though there are others. Stephen J. Gould, a biologist, has written a series of literate essays for the general public, principally about evolution, that look considerably different from the scientific journal article. Gould has broken his generic traditions to "go public" because he already has tenure at Harvard, he likes to write essays, and he enjoys addressing a public audience (see Gould, 1985). Deborah Tannen, an applied linguist, has also "gone public," publishing "pop books" about communication between men and women that are best-sellers in the United States (see Tannen, 1986, 1994). She continues to write relatively conventional articles in journals, but she also writes often for the layperson. Clifford Geertz, the anthropologist, refuses to be pigeon-holed in terms of topic, argumentation, or genre. Using his own disciplinary approaches, he writes texts on academic cultures as well as the "exotic" ones that are typical to anthropologists (see Geertz, 1988). Gould, Tannen, and Geertz have established themselves within their disciplines. Now famous, they can afford to defy community conventions as they write in their individual ways.

Rule breaking is a minefield for many students, however. They first need to understand some of the basic conventions, concepts, and values of a community's genres. Learning and using academic conventions is not easy, for many students receive little or no instruction. To compound the problems, students need constantly to revise their theories of genres and genre conventions (see Bartholomae, 1985). Some graduate students, for example, often express confusion about conventions, anticonventions, and the breaking of rules, for faculty advice appears to be idiosyncratic, based not on community conventions but on personal taste. Some faculty thesis advisers, particularly in the humanities, require a careful review of the literature and accept nothing else; others may insist on "original"[15] work without a literature review. For some advisers there is a "cookie cutter" macrostructure that all papers must follow; others may prefer a more free-flowing, experimental text. Graduate students complain that discovering or breaking these implicit rules requires much research and many visits to faculty offices, as well as many drafts of their thesis chapters (see Schneider & Fujishima, 1995).

It should be clear from this discussion that we cannot tell students "truths" about texts or community practices. However, we can heighten student awareness of generic conventions, and we can assist students in formulating questions that can be addressed to faculty. In our literacy classes, we are developing researchers, not dogmatists, students who explore ideas and literacies rather than seek simple answers.

Dialogue and critique

In any thriving academic community, there is constant dialogue: disagreements among members about approaches to research, about argumentation, about topics for study, and about theory. The journal *Science* acknowledges this and accepts two types of letters to the editor to enable writers to carry out informal dialogues. In other journals, sections are set aside for short interchanges between two writers who hold opposing views (see the *Journal of Second Language Writing,* for example). Most journals carry critiques of new volumes in book review sections, and many published articles are in dialogue with other texts. Academic communities encourage variety and critique (within limits), because that is how they evolve and grow.

Most professional academics know the rules for dialogue: what topics are currently "hot," how to discuss these topics in ways appropriate for the readers of their genres, how far they can go from the current norms, and what they can use (data, narratives, nonlinear texts) to support their arguments. Some professionals who understand the rules can also break them with impunity. They can push the boundaries because they know where the discipline has been and where it may be going, and how to use their authority, and the authority of others, to make their arguments. In a volume on academic expertise, Geisler (1994) comments that there are three "worlds" with which expert academics must be familiar before they can join, or contravene, a disciplinary dialogue: the "domain content world" of logically related concepts and content; the "narrated world" of everyday experience; and the "abstract world" of authorial conversation.

---

15 Since I am arguing here that all texts rely on other texts, I put "original" in quotation marks.

Academic experts must manipulate these worlds in order to produce texts that can be in dialogue or conflict with, yet appropriate to, the communities they are addressing.

This discussion has suggested that communities and their genres are useful to study not only because they can share conventions, values, and histories but because they are evolving: through affiliation of new, different members; through changes in authority; through anticonventionalism, dialogue, and critique. Students know these things about their own communities; we need to draw from this knowledge to begin to explore unfamiliar academic communities and their genres.

This chapter has addressed some of the social and cultural factors that influence texts, factors that are closely related to community membership. Although there is much debate in the literature about the nature of discourse communities and communities of practice, it can be said with some certainty that community affiliations are very real to individual academic faculty. Faculty refer to themselves as "chemists," "engineers," "historians," or "applied linguists"; they read texts from community genres with great interest or join in heated debates with their peers over the Internet. They sometimes recognize that the language, values, and genres of their communities (or specializations) may differ from those of another academic community, though this is not always the case. At a promotions committee made up of faculty from sixteen departments in which I took part, a member of the quantitative group in the Geography Department said of a humanities text, "We shouldn't accept an article for promotion without statistics." And we all laughed, nervously.

Academics, and others, may belong to several communities and have in common certain interests within each. Thus, faculty may have nothing in common with other faculty in their disciplines but the discipline itself; their social, political, and other interests can, and often do, vary widely. In one department, for example, musical interests can be diverse. There may be country-western fans, opera fans, jazz enthusiasts, and those whose only musical experiences consist of listening to the national anthem at baseball games. Recreational interests may also differ. Among faculty, there are motorcyclists and bicyclists, hikers and "couch potatoes," football fans and those who actually play the sport.

A complex of social, community-related factors influences the socioliteracies of faculty and the students who are in their classes. As literacy practitioners, we need to help our students examine these factors by bringing other faculty and students, and their genres, into our classrooms, as well as drawing from our own students' rich resources.

5 Special roles

Literacy practitioners as campus mediators and researchers

The role of literacy in academic life has remained largely transparent – unexamined (Russell, 1991, p. 7).

The development of socioliteracies requires interaction and analysis using a variety of texts, roles, and contexts. If we are to encourage socioliterate practices among our students, we must model for them the ways in which these interactions can take place. We must carve out for ourselves unusual, mediating roles, which ensure collaboration with faculty and administrators, promote student and faculty literacy research, and encourage projects that require all faculty to take responsibility for student literacy growth. There are obstacles to be surmounted in these mediating and research efforts; however, if we promote our goals in ways that are consistent with those of influential faculty and campus administrators, we can recruit powerful partners in our literacy efforts.

This chapter addresses the following questions relating to our roles as mediators within academic contexts:

1. What obstacles stand in the way of involving discipline-specific (DS) faculty in the promotion of socioliteracy?
2. What are some of the ways in which we can involve DS faculty in literacy research?
3. In what ways can literacy and DS faculty join in pedagogical endeavors?
4. How are the WAC/LAC programs designed to promote faculty interest in literacies?

Obstacles to campus innovation

Good teaching unrewarded

In many academic settings, DS faculty are not particularly interested in changing their approaches to teaching in order to improve student literacies or critical thinking. Why is this the case? There are a number of reasons. The first is that faculty tend to behave in their classrooms in ways that are comfortable and familiar. When they were university students, their teachers lectured, so they lecture; their own university classes required textbooks, so they require them as well. They were examined through in-class essays or multiple-choice questions, so they examine their students in the same way. Very little in their educational histories encourages them to question these practices or to ask whether these are the most effective ways to teach or to evaluate their students. Second, for many DS faculty, teaching is less rewarding and motivating than research. Whereas their work in the laboratory, the field, or the library provides the core of their intellectual lives, teaching and learning are not considered to be intellectual activities. Most faculty do not publish about their teaching or student learning; and if they do, these publications often do not assist them in advancing within their disciplines or in their universities. In some universities, the publication of a student textbook can count against faculty in the promotion process rather than for them. They are urged to publish "scholarly" volumes instead. Perhaps the most important reason for the maintenance of traditional and unexamined teaching practices is that on many campuses there is little or no recognition of good teaching. If faculty improve the literate lives of their students by teaching creatively, only the students know. So why should faculty change?

Naive literacy theories

Student literacies have not been, for the most part, intellectually interesting to DS faculty; however, this does not prevent faculty from having opinions on the topic. Complaints about the literacy levels of students are common in all parts of the world, as they always have been. There continue to be two recurring themes in these literacy complaints: One relates to a widespread belief in a "literacy–illiteracy construct," and the other is based on a related "single literacy" view (see McKay, 1993, p. 2). The many faculty who believe in the literacy–illiteracy construct maintain that students are either academically literate or they are not; there is no middle ground. Faculty holding this view say things like "The graduate students in our department are illiterate," or "My students can't read and write." Graduate students are not "illiterate," of course. However, they may need some assistance in reading and writing in the genres of their chosen disciplines and in understanding the values and research practices of their professors. Students in secondary schools and undergraduate programs can read and write, of course; however, they may need help in understanding and developing the kinds of reading and writing that are valued in a particular discipline or classroom or in appropriately editing their work.

Related to this literacy–illiteracy construct is another, widely held conviction among faculty: that there is a single, unified literacy. The proponents of this view believe firmly that at some point in their lives, students can attain a unitary macroskill that will enable them to move immediately from an illiterate to a literate state. Students are viewed as either "remedial" or as sufficiently literate to do university work, and this distinction is generally established, the faculty believe, through a single entrance examination. Thus, Russell notes that most academic faculty and administrators think of writing (and reading) as "generalizable, elementary skill[s]" (1991, p. 7). Those who hold this view believe that illiteracy can be quickly fixed by correcting grammar and mechanics and providing spelling practice or by simple memorization of grammatical paradigms. This "generalizable, elementary" literacy view may help to explain why faculty and administrators believe that one "remedial" or second or foreign language class will be sufficient to stamp out student "illiteracy."[1]

Marginalized literacy faculty

Because literacy and language teaching are not matters of intellectual interest in most academic departments, with the possible exception of education,[2] and because of the widely held simplistic, single literacy view, literacy teaching has been relegated in many institutions to marginalized units with marginalized faculty. This situation is particularly common in English-speaking countries, but it is also true on many campuses in other countries. Literacy teachers tend to be the lowest-status members of English departments or the untenured instructors in language institutes or English for Specific Purposes centers. If the literacy responsibilities are housed in traditional departments of literature or foreign languages, the instructors who are asked to teach composition, reading, or ESL/EFL are often the ones considered insufficiently competent to teach literature.

In some cases, literacy responsibilities are physically moved from campuses to less prestigious locations or units, such as extension divisions, so that the main campus will not be stigmatized by its "illiterate" students, who "can't read or write academic English." These relocated units tend to be self-supporting, expected to recruit students from overseas or from local businesses and prepare them for the university or the professions while at the same time providing additional funding through student

1 Of course, faculty are not alone in the belief that literacy is a simple skill. In a letter to the advice columnist, Ann Landers (*San Diego Union*, January 2, 1996, p. E-2), a personnel manager complained about the illiteracies of college graduates. Ann responded with this comment: "I see the sentence construction and spelling of today's college graduates in my mail every day, and it's depressing." There are other problems with literacy instruction as well. My friend Zakia Sarwar, from Karachi, Pakistan, speaks of writing classes with more than 100 students – and Pakistan is not the only country facing this difficulty.
2 Education is a discipline that some faculty consider "unacademic" because "it has no content." Like many applied linguists, educators are interested in acquisition and process, in methodology and evaluation.

tuition for the campus coffers. As can be seen, then, the most basic academic responsibility, the advancement of literacy and the development of life-long literate practices, is relegated to units that have little or no power, to the "fixers" rather than to the academic leaders and recognized intellectuals. In a discussion of the paradoxes of this situation, Robinson (1983, p. 245) comments that "a fact of life in our world is that the *profession* of literacy, as contrasted with its possession, correlates not with power and wealth but with relative powerlessness and relative poverty."

No single literacy discipline

Other forces also act to marginalize our profession. For example, literacy teaching is, in most cases, not identified with a single, recognized and established international discipline. Thus, it is not "discipline-specific." We literacy practitioners have diverse backgrounds: in literature, in education, in applied linguistics, in foreign language or bilingual teaching, and in composition and rhetoric. Though this diversity undoubtedly enhances our cross-disciplinary consciousness and enriches our teaching, the fact that we do not identify with a single internationally recognized discipline is detrimental to our profession in the eyes of many faculty and administrators. Our "professional diaspora" (Belcher & Braine, 1995) does not promote our cause on many university campuses, where a single textbook, a primary granting agency, or one professional association may identify for many faculty the factors necessary for disciplinary solidarity, identity, and status. When I interviewed electrical engineers about their disciplinary practices, for example, they had no difficulty identifying the basic textbook, the important conferences to attend, the essential granting agencies, and the journals in which it is necessary to publish. Among literacy practitioners, on the other hand, there are separate constituencies, groups that know very little about each other and who seldom read each other's work. In English-speaking countries, those who teach native speakers and attend conferences such as College Composition and Communication know very little about those who teach English as a Second Language (ESL) and bilingual students, and who attend National Association of Bilingual Educators (NABE) conferences or the Teachers of English to Speakers of Other Languages (TESOL) conventions. In English as a Foreign Language (EFL) contexts, the affiliations are somewhat different; in many cases, there are divisions between the literature and the applied linguistics practitioners and between the "common core" English advocates, who believe that there is "one" English, and those who are involved in English for Specific Purposes (ESP) enterprises. Literacy practitioners teach in many different kinds of units. In Malaysia, for example, EFL teaching is often in the Human Resources Division, whereas in other countries, such as Morocco, it is often connected to specific-purpose units such as an institute of agronomy. Thus, we literacy practitioners cannot identify our basic textbooks, and we differ in our pedagogical theories, our conference and organization affiliations, and our teaching units. The fact that we do not speak with a single voice may be one of our greatest strengths; for this reason, however, it is difficult for us to explain ourselves to others on our campuses.

Conflicting faculty values

Our core values, which tend to place pedagogy and language acquisition above content, also separate us from the rest of the campus. One of my own experiences may illustrate this point. Once I attended some critical-thinking workshops for community college and university faculty. In these sessions, ESL, composition, history, and philosophy instructors met in small interest groups and then reported to the whole on pedagogical innovation. Inevitably, the premises with which the ESL and composition groups began their discussions and reports were pedagogical, student- and language-centered. The history and philosophy faculty, on the other hand, were most concerned with organization and presentation of course content. Some of the DS faculty referred to our pedagogical suggestions in demeaning terms such as "little techniques for classrooms." In the eyes of the "academic" teachers, then, the literacy instructors appeared to be unconcerned with the "real stuff" of the university.

In this chapter, I will argue that just because we have often been marginalized and have different goals from other faculty, we must not take the back seat. Instead, we can, and should, take unusual and pivotal roles on our campuses. We should not confine ourselves to grading papers or to our own literacy units and teaching. Instead, we should act as mediators between our students and other instructors and administrators, between what we know about teaching and learning and the academic cultures our students will enter. There is considerable discussion in the literature about "empowering" students (Benesch, 1988; see Johnson & Roen, 1989). If we do not provide personal examples of our own empowering influences on the campus, our students will not take heart. We cannot expect students to research and negotiate, mediate and appropriate texts and situations on the campuses unless these activities are modeled for them.

If we close our classroom doors, believing that we alone can "fix what's wrong" with our students' reading, writing, and critical thinking, then we are, in fact, collaborators with those faculty who perpetuate the reductionist literacy views discussed earlier. If we believe that most disciplinary reading and writing tasks are inferior to the ones we assign, then we will not investigate other texts and tasks with interest. However, if we conceive of academic literacy as evolving, complex, contextualized, and collaborative, a process for which students and faculty must all take responsibility, then we can play important roles in educating faculty, facilitating student literacy development and, while doing so, enhance our own status in our institutions.

Avenues for research: Questionnaires and interviews

In this section I will suggest a few methods by which we literacy teachers can model, research, and mediate, and through our efforts influence the campus while learning more about its disciplines and practices. Drawing from the literature and from my own experiences, I will discuss some possibilities for institutional collaboration in ongoing literacy research and development, mediative efforts that can lead to improved teaching and learning in all classrooms.

Initial interactions: Questionnaires

How can we begin our efforts to mediate between our students and campus faculty? One possibility is to make contacts with academic faculty through questionnaires, an approach that is effective for pedagogical, political, as well as research reasons (Johns, 1981b, 1986). The word *begin* must be emphasized, however, for questionnaires can provide only a first step, an entry into research and pedagogical interaction across the campus. These tools can be used in many and varied ways, depending on our purposes and goals and their place within our research continuum. They can be used to assist literacy practitioners in developing their curricula as well as in demonstrating to faculty a commitment to literacy. For example, in the Sudan, an EFL context, Markee (1986) attempted to discover how English and Arabic were being used in classrooms across campus in order to design more appropriate literacy curricula. He found that his needs assessment questionnaires (and follow-up interviews) were adequate to determine the "formal system," the ways languages were intended to be used on his campus in the Sudan. However, only through observation and interviews could he determine the "informal system" of language use: what actually happened linguistically in DS classrooms.

In environments where English is the sole medium of instruction, there may be other purposes for distributing questionnaires among faculty. One can be to determine which "skills" are most important to students at a particular level – reading, writing, speaking, or listening – in order to establish emphases within a literacy curriculum. With this purpose in mind, I distributed a simple questionnaire to 200 instructors at my university, a randomly selected 10 percent of the faculty population (Johns,

1981b). The questionnaire was accompanied by a letter from the International Committee on campus, a group whose members had considerable prestige. The results, which we distributed to interested faculty and administrators, were useful, though not surprising. For undergraduate students, reading was considered to be the most important of the four skills, listening was the second most important, writing was third (19 percent), and speaking came last. Among graduate faculty, the responses were different: writing (the thesis or dissertation) was considered most important, and speaking was highly valued. This skills survey has been replicated in EFL contexts with similar results. Hohl (1982), for example, found that at the University of Petroleum and Minerals (Saudi Arabia), reading and listening were ranked first and second for undergraduates, with textbook reading and note taking identified as most important.

As can be seen from the dates of the publications cited in this section, campus questionnaires may not be as common as they once were, perhaps because they are difficult to publish or because they cannot fully expose the problematic and complex nature of literacy practices.[3] However, there continue to be important reasons for creating and distributing these instruments on our campuses. One is to elicit written commentary on students and their literacies from a larger number of faculty. Through questionnaires, we can also request sample assignments and model papers, all of which can be helpful in designing curricula (see Horowitz, 1986a). In addition, we can identify those faculty who might be interested in follow-up interviews or cooperative research and teaching. A final, not trivial reason for designing faculty questionnaires is to publicize the work of the literacy unit to the university, to show that our interests are closely allied to the concerns of the faculty and administrators.

Faculty interviews

Other mediation and research efforts can be made through interviews. Interviews can have a number of goals, most of which parallel those for questionnaires; however, the type of data collected is considerably different. One important purpose for interviews is questionnaire follow-up: to gain additional insights into how and why faculty responded in certain ways. Another purpose is to make discoveries about a particular class in a discipline, a single site for the development of literacy practices. Because each classroom is different from every other, for a variety of reasons, such single-site research assists us in maintaining a balance between our generalizations about literacies and the particulars of rhetori-

---

3 They are still widely used as needs assessments in English for Specific Purposes contexts, particularly in developing business curricula. See Barbara et al. (1996), Khoo (1993), and Pang and Heng (1993).

cal situation. In the following sections, I will discuss three of the many purposes that interviews can serve within an academic context.

ON CLASSROOM GOALS AND MANAGEMENT

As is discussed at some length in later chapters, our campus has established a program in which literacy and DS classes are linked: The same cohort of students enroll in the DS class and in the literacy class. When one of these links has been established, the DS instructor and the literacy faculty often exchange syllabi and then sit down to discuss their goals for students.[4] Dialogic interviews of this type need not be restricted to faculty in linked class contexts; any faculty who want a literacy expert to examine their syllabus and help them with their teaching practices may benefit from a literacy interview, particularly if it is followed by some concrete advice.

Here are some questions that can be posed to DS faculty as syllabi are exchanged.

- What does critical thinking mean for your class or your discipline? What critical thinking, reading, and writing objectives do you have for students? What would you like students to be able to do in these areas that they cannot do when they enter your class?
- What kinds of readings are you assigning? From textbooks? From other sources? How do you want students to approach the reading of these texts? Are they to read the various texts differently?
- What kinds of writing do you require? What should students know or be able to do when they write? What do the essay examination questions look like? How else do you use writing in your classes? Do you require any uncorrected writing, such as "quick writes?"
- Do you administer a needs assessment to your students? If so, what have you discovered about their linguistic backgrounds or their understanding of the discipline? Do they understand your reading and writing demands?
- Can I, as a literacy instructor, be of use to you in your class? For example, can I help students to work in groups to complete their projects? Can I ask them questions (with you present) about how they read for your assignments?
- Would you be willing to come to my literacy class to discuss examples of good and poor writing taken from the students' own work? Would you be willing to talk to them about why you became involved in your

---

4 As some readers will predict, not all DS instructors are willing to sit down and chat about these matters; however, because the linked classes have become the norm for our first-year students, faculty appear to be more interested in cooperative efforts.

discipline and to show the students some examples of your research efforts?

These questions open up possibilities for discussion of literacy issues that faculty may not have considered: defining critical thinking for a class, noticing the variety of reading and writing strategies required, and identifying good (and poor) work for a specific assignment. The questions also encourage continuous interaction between literacy instructors and DS faculty. Through these interviews, faculty come to appreciate our expertise: our abilities to analyze texts, to discuss language use, and to identify critical thinking demands.

AS FOLLOW-UP

It is also important to keep in contact with DS faculty, to let them know that their views of the world, however painful to us at times, are important to us and to our students. One year, when I asked the DS instructor whose class was linked to mine how our students were doing, he made a predictable response: that the students were "illiterate." Rather than slitting my wrists or branding him as simplistic, I viewed this comment as an opportunity for a follow-up interview. During the interview, he identified specific reading, writing, and critical-thinking practices that were expected in his classroom, but not evident to him in student work (Johns, 1991). We discussed how the goals and pedagogy for both the students' DS and literacy classes might be revised to enhance student practices and to improve their literacies. The results of this interview have been distributed to other faculty in meetings and workshops to encourage discussion beyond the "single skill" literacy hypothesis.

Interviews such as this, conducted after faculty members complain about student "illiteracy," can lead to other types of interactions with faculty and administrators. Interviews provide opportunities to ask faculty to reconsider how they present assignments and conduct their classes. They give us opportunities to encourage faculty to reevaluate their criteria for assessment. They may also give us opportunities to distribute some of the many pedagogical guides for faculty that appear in the literature.

ABOUT SPECIFIC CURRICULAR ISSUES

It is important to conduct general literacy research through questionnaires and interviews, but our research can, and should, be directed at specific literacy issues as well. In one set of interviews conducted in the College of Engineering, I had narrow objectives in mind (Johns, 1993). "Improving argumentation" was listed as a goal in my class syllabus, but my electrical engineering students and I understood very little about academic argumentation and audiences in their chosen discipline.

With this in mind, I visited two bilingual[5] electrical engineering faculty to explore the genres and argumentation that were valued in their discipline. These experts told me that the most important "named" professional genre was not the research article, as is the case in many disciplines, but the grant proposal (see also Connor, 1996, pp. 134–135). Throughout my interview with the two professors, argumentation and audience analysis were identified as the key elements for a successful grant proposal. In our discussion, we turned to these engineers' discipline-specific approaches to claims, data, and warrants in argumentation (Toulmin, 1958), and the nonlinear texts (graphs, charts, formulas) that are, for them, more important to argumentation than written discourses. The credibility I gained with students from these interviews has been considerable, in addition to the obvious research and teaching benefits.

Teaching implications: Questionnaires and interviews

It is important to note here that the use of questionnaires and interviews, and the collection and discussion of texts and literacy practices, can affect literacy instruction directly. For example, interviews with faculty can counteract student theories of classroom texts as autonomous, removed from the communities and situations in which they are produced. After we talk to DS faculty, our understanding of the complexities of text processing and production can encourage us, and our students, to conceive of texts as rhetorically and linguistically motivated and to assess literacy practices in various situations. For, as Chiseri-Strater tells us, "Poor writing (or reading) for the novice in the field . . . is often not the result of deficient skills but rather the result of the new context and language in the field the students are working in" (1991, p. 69).

As can be seen, our goals in interacting with academic faculty and professionals in distributing questionnaires or conducting interviews can be several: to develop a better understanding of the characteristics of DS classroom literacy tasks and expectations, to be exposed to disciplinary communities and the texts from genres that these cultures value, to bring our interests and concerns to the attention of DS faculty, to increase faculty awareness of student linguistic and educational diversity, to begin collaboration on research and teaching projects, and not incidentally, to design more appropriate literacy curricula. Research with faculty undoubtedly enriches our status and professional lives and changes the attitudes and practices that we bring to literacy classrooms.

---

5 Their first languages were Chinese (Mandarin) and Japanese.

Joint pedagogical endeavors

There are other, more direct avenues for interacting with faculty and their communities, several of which fall under the "Content-Based Instruction" (CBI) rubric in the United States, but in other parts of the world might be called "Language-across-the-Curriculum" (LAC) or English for Academic Purposes (EAP). In their widely disseminated volume entitled *Content-Based Second Language Instruction,* Brinton, Snow, and Wesche (1989) describe three CBI program models: adjunct (or linked), sheltered, and theme-based, all of which encourage close ties between curricular content and objectives of the disciplines and the development of student literacy practices. Eskey (1992, pp. 17–18) notes that the content-based syllabus in a literacy classroom "provides a kind of natural continuity [among language, function, and content], creates genuine occasions for use of these . . . for negotiating meaning, and tends to pull all three dimensions of language learning together around a particular communicative goal."

The questions addressed here are these: How can CBI programs reach out beyond the literacy classroom? How can they become integral to a cross-disciplinary discussion and pedagogy that will be of general benefit to our students? Some CBI models may help us to answer these questions.

Team teaching

The most collaborative of CBI structures is team teaching. Though it is seldom practiced in the United States or in EFL contexts, this approach is well known in the United Kingdom because it has been in place at the University of Birmingham for more than 20 years. This CBI approach is quite rare because it is considered too difficult or too expensive to manage within most academic environments. John Swales, introducing the Johns and Dudley-Evans (1980) article on team teaching in *Episodes in ESP,* warns that "approaches such as this achieve their considerable and impressive purposes only by considerable and impressive expenditure of time and effort on behalf of restricted numbers of students" (Swales, 1988a, p. 138). Nonetheless, it is important to discuss the objectives and foci of team teaching, for this approach is in many ways the ideal. In addition, the activities employed in the Birmingham model can be adapted to other CBI approaches such as the adjunct (linked), sheltered, or theme-based models.

When establishing their program, Johns and Dudley-Evans identified a science instructor who was interested in working directly with literacy instructors to improve students' academic proficiencies. In the planning stage, the literacy staff met frequently with the science instructor to determine what elements of the target students' coursework were most obviously in need of improvement and amenable to literacy instruction. The Birmingham team decided to focus in the literacy class on lecture comprehension and note taking during the students' first semester, and on writing essay examinations in the second semester. The instructors also assisted the science instructor in improving his teaching approaches and assignments to make them more appropriate and accessible to the ESL student population.

During the first term, the following goals are pursued in the literacy class:

1. Developing global understanding through rearrangement of major points in the lecture, identifying the overall argument of the lecture and classifying the evidence used
2. Identifying and classifying the detail (e.g., terms and their characteristics)
3. Identifying and using technical and subtechnical vocabulary (Johns & Dudley-Evans, 1980, reprinted in Swales, 1988a, pp. 144–150)

What the authors describe for this first semester can be goals for many literacy programs. Certainly, the approach used here to lectures – augmented perhaps by the work of Olsen and Huckin (1990), DeCarrico and Nattinger (1988), Flowerdew (1995), and Lebauer (1984) – should be of considerable use in less elaborate and time-consuming literacy ventures.

The second-semester course in the Birmingham team-teaching program should also be of general interest to literacy practitioners. In this term the focus is on essay examination questions. Initially, the subject instructor sets the questions and discusses criteria for good responses with the literacy instructors. In the literacy classes, instructors assist students in (Johns & Dudley Evans, 1980, reprinted in Swales, 1988a, pp. 150–151):

1. Understanding the question through analyzing the form–function correspondences (for *definition,* "Define")
2. Understanding the examiner's intentions and expectations as they relate to the goals of the subject course [This involves a review of the conceptual framework of the course. See also Mohan, 1986, pp. 25–51]
3. Preparing a response through structuring the information for the argument through review of lecture notes and the textbook
4. Relating the response to the course framework
5. Making decisions about answer presentation, for example, ordering of points and paragraphing

Under this team-teaching arrangement, the literacy and the DS instructors attend each other's class sessions throughout the term. In his classroom, the science teacher makes an effort to "shelter" his language and assignments, speaking more slowly and assigning carefully outlined tasks. The literacy teacher then works with the students in a separate class to achieve the specific language and proficiency goals agreed upon by the team.

In discussing this program, the authors explain what must seem evident: that the approach leads to an important partnership between DS and literacy instructors, one in which teaching in both the literacy class and the DS class is carefully evaluated and improved. Though it is difficult to replicate, the Birmingham model for team teaching embodies many of the important elements to which all socioliteracy programs can aspire: collaboration between DS and literacy instructors, concentration on identified student needs, use of authentic classroom discourses, and a focus on specific literacies required in DS classrooms.

Linked (adjunct) programs

The discussion now turns to a CBI program structure that is more common, principally because it is feasible within a large variety of academic contexts. Linked (or adjunct) programs exist throughout the world in a variety of forms.[6] On our campus, we have been offering linked classes since 1985 in what we call the Integrated Curriculum (IC). In recent years, IC linked classes have become central components in our Freshman Success Programs, which include a General Education class (GE) such as biology, history, psychology, or literature, a study group for the GE class, a writing (literacy) class, a campus orientation class (University Seminar), and, for some students, a special dormitory (see Figure 1).

Over the years, DS faculty have begun to request linked class arrangements because they find that students in these programs are better prepared for their GE classes than those who are not "linked." Those DS faculty whose classes are dropped from the linked program are often unhappy, asking, "Wasn't I good enough?" It has become an honor to be asked to teach a linked GE class within the Integrated Curriculum.

How is a linked (or adjunct) class designed? The basic components are an authentic, unchanged DS class, such as Introduction to Biology or Principles of Economics, and a literacy (writing) course in which a student cohort from the GE class is enrolled. Often the GE course is a large lecture and/or laboratory class; the literacy class cohort represents about

6 Our campus, like several others, has chosen to use the term "linked," because "adjunct" implies that literacy instruction is subordinate to the work of the DS classes.

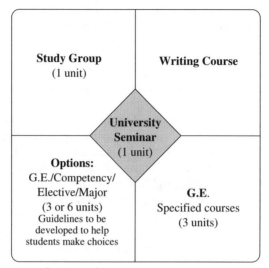

Figure 1   Integrated curriculum.

25 percent of the lecture class enrollment. In many contexts, additional components are included in the linked program. In the UCLA Freshman Summer program, described by Brinton et al. (1989, pp. 57–69), dormitory and social events are included. In the Freshman Success Program on our campus, the linked GE and literacy courses are combined, when possible, with a residential life segment (many of the students live in the same dormitory) and include academic and personal counseling.

Collaborative efforts among faculty from the DS and literacy classes, though not required, often occur on an informal basis. Gee (1992), a literacy teacher in what are called "special paired" or "connected" classes at a community college, asks the DS instructors to complete a questionnaire about assignments and classroom expectations before the term begins (pp. 89–92). Using this tool, the two instructors discuss their goals and syllabi, and schedule times at which they can visit each other's classes. In our university's Freshman Success Program, we also attempt to meet with the DS faculty to discuss syllabi and shared goals. We invite faculty to attend our literacy classes as experts or to talk about how they became interested in their disciplines, teaching, or research. As a result of these efforts, some faculty consult us about their textbook choices and the wording of their examinations, about how they can manage their classes more effectively (particularly using group work), or about what we might do cooperatively for a student who is not performing well. Faculty also make changes in their approaches to content and assignments, as we "critically intervene" on behalf of the students (Benesch,

1996). The students in our linked classes can also be involved in this partnership, sometimes in unusual ways. At one point, when literacy students enrolled in a linked biology class felt that an assigned book was too difficult, they ran a readability check of the text on one of our department computers. After seeing the results of this measure (a very high reading level), the biology professor laughed, promised the students that he would explain the book more carefully in class, and then decided to require an alternative volume for future classes.

Thus, though a linked (adjunct) class model may not always lend itself structurally to the cooperative efforts found in the team-teaching approaches, it can lead to informal cooperation among the faculty (and students), particularly if the literacy specialists take the lead in creating a teaching team. Linked classes also have one distinct advantage over team-teaching and the other common CBI models, sheltered English and theme-based: The discipline-specific courses are absolutely authentic and unsheltered. Faculty in DS classes teach and evaluate as they have always done, unless, of course, they can be encouraged to modify their approaches to encourage more effective literacy development.[7] This reality therapy is good for students, who must contend with what is really out there, however difficult that may be.

The linked and team-teaching models appear to be one of the most effective pedagogical approaches to raising DS faculty awareness because, if they are at all interested in improving their teaching, their interests will be directed toward their own disciplines and their own classes in these models. During the past decade or so, campus literacy faculty have found that by working with faculty in linked arrangements, we can be effective advisers and campus change agents. When faculty have good experiences with linked classes and pedagogical change, they go back to their own departments and colleagues and spread the word. Sometimes they hold workshops for other faculty to show them how they have innovated while in linked arrangements; sometimes they write about (or co-author, with us) their innovations. For the most part, however, the word is spread informally, and it has authority because it comes from DS faculty colleagues.

Other models: Sheltered and theme-based

Two other important models for CBI are sheltered English and theme-based. In sheltered programs, students who need language or other aca-

7 M. Ann Snow, at California State University, Los Angeles, uses a grant from the Fund for the Improvement of Secondary Education (FIPSE) to work with faculty for an entire year on developing curricula for specific classes that support linguistically diverse students. She can be contacted through the College of Education, CSU Los Angeles.

demic support are separated from other students and given a special class, generally taught by a faculty expert. Several modifications are made for the student population:

> For example, texts are carefully selected for their organization and clarity; the instructor might gear lectures more closely to the written text and make certain linguistic adjustments to allow for students' listening comprehension difficulties, and the overall course requirements might be altered to include greater emphasis on receptive skills and less on speaking and writing (Brinton et al., 1989, p. 16).

In theme-based classes, which are becoming increasingly common in primary, secondary, and university classes throughout the world, "the language class is structured around topics or themes, with topics forming the basis for the classroom curriculum" (Brinton et al., 1989, p. 14). As theme-based classes have been mandated in various schools and as literacy instructors realize how useful a central theme can be, these models have become increasingly sophisticated (see Rosen, 1992). Of particular use for those interested in a theme-based program should be the suggestions by Bernard Mohan (1986, pp. 25–52), who demonstrates how knowledge, concepts, and language can be integrated; and the work of Stoller and Grabe (1995), who have introduced the "Six T's" into CBI curriculum design: general theme, topics (or subthemes), tasks, texts, transitions from topic to topic, and threads (the weaving of one content area into another).

Sheltered and theme-based approaches are easier to execute administratively than team-teaching or linked (adjunct) classes. They can be beneficial to students, particularly if they make use of some of the socioliterate principles advocated in this volume. Good literacy instructors, whatever the model, present to students a variety of texts and tasks and introduce them to some of the diverse socioliterate practices of the disciplines. These teachers make use of content experts, and they integrate language, reading and writing, concepts, and critical thinking. Thus, though team teaching or linked classes are the optimal, the other CBI models, if well executed, can also be effective in advancing student literacies.

Writing (Language)-across-the-Curriculum programs

The Writing-across-the-Curriculum (WAC)[8] and Language-across-the-Curriculum (LAC) movements are devoted to encouraging faculty to

---

8 Now, more commonly called "Writing in the Disciplines" (see Herrington & Moran, 1992).

reconsider and revise their teaching. The LAC movement, initiated in Great Britain, has traditionally focused on language development, with no artificial separation between language proficiency growth and "language for learning" (Martin, 1992). Since the movement's inception in the mid-1970s, LAC advocates have been concerned with the education of linguistically and culturally diverse students, particularly in content classes at the primary and secondary levels. Thus the emphasis is on early language development and the registers of particular content areas such as the sciences and social sciences. The WAC movement has been most evident at the postsecondary level in the United States, at community (two-year) colleges as well as at universities. In WAC, the principal emphasis has been on writing, since composition is the one "skill" that is taught and tested at a number of academic levels. The majority of the WAC programs in the United States are housed in English departments, directed by composition instructors who are most comfortable with native speakers of English. The WAC directors and their staff hold workshops for DS faculty on writing and assessment issues or consult with individual faculty about their classroom concerns. Unfortunately, literacy teachers of linguistically and culturally diverse students have, for the most part, been excluded from the WAC programs. As student populations become more multilingual and as the importance of integrating reading and writing becomes more accepted in the United States, these instructors should try to take an active part in WAC/LAC programs at every level, for they have much to offer these programs.

In EFL contexts, where official WAC/LAC movements are less in evidence, there are various types of formal and informal cross-curricular programs in which literacy instructors and faculty from the disciplines cooperate to improve English language literacy, conduct research, or train junior teachers. I have witnessed the workings of several such programs, perhaps the most impressive of which is the interaction between literacy and engineering at Blida University (Algeria), in which the DS faculty, educated in English-speaking countries, teach the language and conventions of their disciplines to their own student majors, employing literacy faculty as consultants. In Europe, a variety of models are in place. At the École Superior Cachon, near Paris, for example, an ESP teacher training course has been established that involves cooperative research, co-teaching, and the preparation of French-speaking faculty and graduate students for English-medium conferences. At ESADE, in Barcelona, literacy faculty work with the faculty in the business school in preparing and delivering lectures in the graduate program, taught completely in English. An extensive cross-curricular program has been in place over the years at the Pontifícia Universidade Católica de São Paulo (Brazil), as often discussed in its publication, *The ESPecialist,* and there are several innovative programs in Chile, Argentina, and Venezuela as well. In China, much cross-campus activity takes place at the technical and business universities, where literacy faculty exert an important influence over the curricula, teaching practices, and examinations.

One WAC experience

When a vacancy occurred, I requested the opportunity to direct our campus WAC program, and I did so for several years. Believing that a discussion of my experience may be useful in contexts elsewhere, I will present some features of this program, particularly as they relate to the role of literacy instructor as mediator within a university.

These were the program goals for our campus:

1. To diversify pedagogical approaches in content classes
2. To increase faculty awareness of student needs, strategies, and difficulties when approaching academic content
3. To encourage faculty to let students in on the "secrets" of their disciplines, the ways of viewing the world, the values, the genres, and the conventions
4. To encourage faculty to make explicit the implicit "rules" of the classroom, by modeling reading and writing processes, by displaying and discussing good student texts, and by focusing on why these texts reflect the values and conventions of the class
5. To promote an intellectual interest in literacy issues among all faculty and administrators on campus, and, not incidentally, to raise the status of literacy faculty

Initially, I conducted traditional WAC workshops, introducing techniques to faculty for modeling reading and writing tasks, for writing-to-learn such as "quick writes," and for developing assessment practices more amenable to the student diversity on our campus. However, these workshops were often misinterpreted as training in "little techniques" rather than in what had been intended: to encourage faculty to make a greater effort to bridge the gap between their expert literacies and the novice literacies of students.

These early experiences caused me to reassess my approach to the WAC program. Now, my literacy colleagues and I work with others on campus to design materials and projects to meet specific needs. Here are a few examples.

1. Faculty from one department were concerned about how they could group their students in large classes. Drawing from the insights of the Cooperative Learning Movement, we worked with them to develop a

step-by-step procedure for establishing groups, writing appropriate group problem-solving activities and maintaining the groups throughout the semester.

2. Faculty from a number of departments asked that a critical-thinking discussion group be established. It was, and we met monthly over lunch to discuss this topic.

3. Another faculty member complained that his students did not understand what was required in essay examination responses. Together, we developed a process by which students responded to a sample prompt. The student responses he identified as "good" and "bad" were then duplicated by the instructor. He distributed these examples to the students without comment, and then the students worked in groups, deciding which responses were the best ones – and why. The group leaders reported on their findings to the class, and then the instructor read the responses that he considered good aloud, discussing why these were appropriate to class goals, concepts, and argumentation.

4. Because there has been a considerable interest in portfolios for curriculum and assessment on our campus, a faculty member decided that he would attempt a portfolio in his class for future teachers of history. We worked together on a plan, and then, as he executed it, we consulted periodically.

5. Seeing the need for a cross-campus discussion of portfolios, one of my colleagues developed a collection of portfolio artifacts and interviews with faculty using portfolios in a number of disciplines.

6. The Graduate Division and several graduate advisers have been concerned about the difficulties faced by bilingual students in completing theses. After considerable discussion, we instituted a workshop class in which students are assisted in preparing for their theses.

7. Most recently, our Dean of Undergraduate Studies has created a computer-generated chat group on teaching for faculty, staff, and administrators throughout the university. After initial predictable complaints about student "illiteracies," the discussants began to talk about specific issues in teaching and testing.

8. Finally, in our Integrated Curriculum Program, we designed an orientation class called University Seminar, taught by faculty, staff (such as directors of counseling and housing), and administrators (including two vice-presidents and most of the college deans). The group meets monthly to discuss concerns: about curriculum, about students, about college teaching, and other issues. These meetings provide an excellent, nonthreatening venue in which to bring out issues of student literacies and the many factors that influence it.

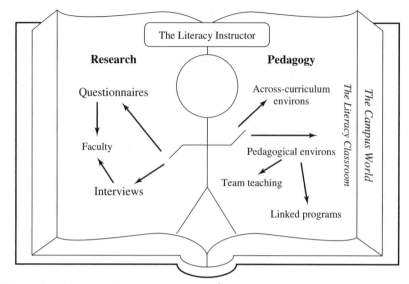

Figure 2   Literacy instructors as mediators.

In this chapter I have argued that as literacy faculty, we must step away from our student papers and out of our classrooms to involve others on our campus in our literacy enterprise. I have suggested questionnaires and interviews, content-based models (CBI), and WAC/LAC programs as some of our mediating possibilities (see Figure 2). I would be unwise and inaccurate, however, to suggest that literacy faculty can establish and maintain these efforts single-handedly. We know better. But we can provide the incentives, the questions, and the starting places. We can appeal to the best in our colleagues, and we can advertise our shared successes. On our campus, we have publicized our expertise through the various newsletters and e-mail routes available to us. We have published written suggestions for improving teaching and learning to a broad spectrum of faculty and administrators. We have served on campus committees in which issues of literacy are raised; we have circulated our literacy research and started various discussion groups; we have offered our expertise to those who request it. We are always on the lookout for opportunities to continue our cross-campus literacy campaigns. When the founder of our WAC program, housed in the Department of English and Comparative Literature, left the campus, we offered to continue it. When a grant proposal for improving the retention of so-called remedial students appeared, we proposed the linked class program that has now become the norm for our first-year students. Our literacy faculty serve on the University Senate, one of the major policy-making bodies on campus.

In all of our efforts, we have sought support from the administration and from faculty in all departments. We share many of their goals, such as student retention, academic literacy advancement, and graduation of literate professionals, and we work cooperatively to achieve these goals. Literacy faculty on other campuses tell us that powerful administrators block their cross-campus efforts or that DS faculty are not interested in improving student literacy. We have such faculty and administrators as well. However, we seek out the people who want to be positive leaders, who will see our joint efforts as beneficial to the campus, to students, and not incidentally, to the furtherance of their personal aims.

Efforts of this type can be made on any campus. When I was visiting a campus in France, a university administrator told me that he needed one more accomplishment to go on his record, so he worked with literacy faculty to found an English for Specific Purposes program. He benefitted personally, but so did the campus and its students. We need to appeal to the interests of our administration and faculty so that everyone benefits in the literacy effort.

The road to improved student socioliteracies through campus mediation is filled with potholes. Over the years, we have experienced many failures and disappointments, but we focus on our successes, on the positive effects that our cooperative efforts have had on our students and the campus climate. We are proud of what we have done, but, of course, there is much more to do.

6 *Students as researchers*
Investigating texts, processes, and contexts

To analyze school or university writing in the light of the recent reconception of genre is a *demystifying* move, in that it, for instance, affords explanations of conventional forms that previously appeared arcane or arbitrary. The effect, however, is to make both the texts and the pedagogical issues look more complex than before (Freedman & Medway, 1994b, p. 12).

We need to bring students to the point of cultural self-consciousness in which they neither accommodate nor merely oppose the social order – both positions being still circumscribed by the structure – but can actively position themselves within it (Herndl, 1993, p. 215).

The most important factor in the success of any pedagogy is the student. Unless we can motivate our students, providing them with tools and experiences that are relevant to their current and future lives outside of our literacy classrooms, we are not doing our jobs. Though we cannot hope to predict all of their possible literacy experiences, we can help students to ask questions of texts, of contexts, of experts – and of themselves. By opening our literacy classroom doors to a variety of possibilities within text worlds and text processing, we can collaborate with students as they acquire an enriched understanding of the challenges, possibilities, and problems for their literate academic and professional lives.

This chapter is devoted to student research. I use the term, "research" broadly, as I did in the previous chapter, to refer to the investigation of a problem or question of interest. Some of what is discussed here could be referred to as "critical thinking" or effective group work; undoubtedly, one of the many benefits of encouraging students to become researchers is that they have much to talk, read, and write about within their literacy classes. However, the activities suggested in this chapter are more focused: They are designed specifically to encourage ongoing student inquiry into texts and genres, their own literate lives, and the literacy practices of others, so that they may be better prepared to position themselves within academic and other social contexts.

Student research and reflection will be continuing themes throughout the remainder of the volume. To begin the discussion, the following questions will be addressed:

1. How can students use texts as catalysts for enquiry? How can they learn from genre exemplars about text-internal properties?
2. What are some of the text-external features of genres that students might explore?
3. How can we promote student inquiry into the processes and strategies they use to complete reading and writing tasks? How can we encourage them to use their research to expand their strategy repertoires?
4. What are some of the class-external research projects that students can conduct? How can they use interviews and participant observation to achieve their ends?

Text-based research

The genre: An examination prompt

If students can learn to view the various features of texts as purposeful rather than arbitrary, as situated and generic rather than autonomous, then they can begin to see how texts fit into a broader social context: of a classroom, a disciplinary community, or a larger culture. They may also begin to understand how considering the social factors that influence texts can enhance their own task representations and processing. This developing student sophistication should promote opportunities to go beyond accommodation to an assignment, into reformulation, negotiation, or resistance within literacy contexts, all of which can be quite successful under certain conditions (see Leki, 1995).

In preparation for text-based research, one or more exemplars from the same genre should be collected, if possible. If a text artifact chosen for study is long, such as a faculty member's dissertation or a university catalog, one example may suffice, at least temporarily. However, if students are examining shorter texts, such as course syllabi or brief textbook readings, it is important to collect several exemplars in order to compare them.

This section uses as a genre exemplar an essay examination prompt, because it is a ubiquitous pedagogical genre and because there is considerable professional research on prompts from which to draw. In one prompt research project, my literacy students, all of whom were enrolled in a cultural geography class,[1] began their research by collecting from the instructor two take-home examination prompts from a previous semester. These texts had been distributed 4 and 8 weeks into the term, 2 weeks

---

1 My students are, for the most part, in linked class arrangements. However, this research can also be conducted with students who are enrolled in different DS classes. Each student then brings in examples of prompts, and the examples are compared.

before in-class examinations. Each examination response was to be written under the same general conditions:

Your essays are to be approximately 500 words in length and type-written using double-spacing. You will hand in your essay at the beginning of class on (date). The essay counts toward 30% of your exam grade. [Note: The remainder of your grade will be determined by an in-class objective and short-answer test.]

These are the two prompts:[2]

Prompt 1: (a) Currently, the world's population of 5.6 billion people is growing at an annual rate of 1.7%. (b) This rate of growth places incredible pressures on the earth's natural resource system and has major impacts on the quality of life for all of its inhabitants, human and otherwise. (c) Discuss the four main perspectives on world population growth, stressing the main themes, what the adherents of each perspective view as the problem, the strong points and limitations of each approach. (d) As a citizen of the planet, which perspectives do you most agree with and why?

Prompt 2: (a) Illegal international migration between Mexico and the United States has commanded a great deal of attention from policy makers in both countries during this century. (b) A sound policy needs to be grounded in an understanding of the magnitude of the flows as well as the forces that generate this form of migration. (c) In your essay, you are to assume the role of a policy analyst who is responsible for providing this information and a discussion of the impacts of this migration on both countries. (d) Additionally, you are to suggest a plan of action for the United States government to shape its immigration policy towards Mexico as well as justification for the policy which you suggest.

Like most texts, these prompts can be analyzed for tense, aspect, syntax, and other text-internal features. They can be studied for cohesive elements (see Halliday & Hasan, 1976), which are particularly important to Prompt 2 ("this information"). And there are other possibilities as well. Three research possibilities using these sample prompts will be presented here.

OUTLINING MOVES

When processing a situated text, readers are said to use mental models based on their schemata, which are then revised as they read or write for the particular situation (see Gernsbacher, 1990; Gordon & Hanauer, 1995). Examining the macrostructure of texts can assist students in developing mental models, which they can later instantiate and revise when confronted with texts of the same genre. To study text macrostructure, my students worked in groups to discover the purposes of the moves within the prompts.

2 Marking the sentences with letters is my addition.

During their analyses, the students discovered that the geography instructor employed predictable moves in his two prompts. He used the first sentences to introduce a topic or present a problem. Thus, sentences (a) and (b) in both examples frame a problem and state a particular point of view toward it. The students discovered that the remainder of both texts is devoted to direct instructions to students: whom they are to be (their roles), and the topics about which they are to write. In Prompt 1, students are to present the basic views on population growth presented in the course, noting "main themes, what the adherents . . . view as the problem, and the strong points and limitations of each approach."[3] They are then to take a role, "as a citizen of the planet," and indicate which of these views they support.

In Prompt 2, the problem is posed and a comment about "sound policy" is made in the first two sentences. Then in sentences (c) and (d), the contextual constraints are set: Students are to take a predetermined role (policy analyst) and write for a particular audience (U.S. government officials). Sentence (d) was thought by the students to be particularly demanding, because it required both the formulation and justification of a suggested plan.

A student investigation of the moves in the macrostructure of two or more texts is a useful exercise. In this case, the students discovered that their professor arranged moves in his prompts in similar ways. This led them to hypothesize that individual faculty may have organizational preferences, a consideration that can help them in their future attempts to understand and respond to prompts. Second, the students discovered that they could take their findings about moves and apply them to prompts from other classes and disciplines, noting not only similarities but differences. To encourage this transfer of learning, I asked them to collect prompts from other classes. Here is one (Prompt 3), from an introductory biology class, written, of course, by a different DS faculty member.

Prompt 3 (30 pts): (a) Discuss the Kingdom Fungi in regards [sic] to some of the salient characteristics contained in the Kingdom; (b) also name some of the Divisions and why their members are important to man, (c) and provide a brief narrative concerning symbioses encountered within this group of organisms.

In this text, the students found no framing of the problem or instructor view of the situation as they had in Prompts 1 and 2. Instead, the prompt moved immediately into instructions for writing. According to the students enrolled in biology classes, the prompt fit very well into their study of scientific taxonomies because in writing a response to this prompt, they were to draw first from the largest taxonomic category ("King-

---

3 Fortunately, the students had been constructing a concept map for the course, so they had quick access to these views in their notes.

dom"), then from a smaller category ("Divisions"), and finally to focus on one central characteristic of the Kingdom, "symbioses." The differences between the moves in these cultural geography and biology prompts are considerable, reflecting, among other things, the conceptual frameworks of the disciplines represented.

ANALYZING GENERIC FEATURES: INSTRUCTIONS

In examination prompts, and in other genres, there tend to be certain conventions, features that help expert readers and writers to process the texts successfully. In almost every examination prompt, for example, we find instructions for the reader of some type, often represented by instructional verbs. When the students reexamined the three prompts from cultural geography and biology, they found these instructional verbs: *discuss* (from 1, 2, and 3); *name* (3); and *suggest* (2). However, they also found instructions in other parts of the prompts. In Prompt 1, for instance, instructions are embedded in a question that asks them to take a stand: "As a citizen of the planet, which perspectives do you agree with and why?" In Prompt 2, sentences (d) and (e), instructions are found in these phrases: "providing information," "a discussion of impacts," and "justification for the policy which you suggest." Thus it is useful for students to study not only the instructional verbs, but directions that are embedded in other grammatical features as well.

Despite the complicating issues discussed above, it is useful to devote time to a study of instructional verbs to ferret out the generic features of prompts and the problems these features can pose. One problem is that some instructional verbs are vague. Researchers tell us, for example, that certain verbs, such as *describe* and *discuss*, must be carefully analyzed for meaning within the context. In a useful article entitled "Essay Examination Prompts and the Teaching of Academic Writing," in which he provides a taxonomy of prompt task categories,[4] Horowitz (1986b, p. 108) notes that, in the following prompts, "describe" has different meanings:

Describe the causes of the War of 1812 (historical causes).
Describe the technologies associated with horticulture and also those associated with agriculture (a listing and perhaps physical description).
Describe the relationship between population growth, urbanization, and the demographic transition (showing interrelationships among concepts).

It is beneficial to students to work with *describe* or *discuss* instructions such as these so that they will be aware of some of the ambiguities they

---

4 Horowitz (1986b, p. 110) divides prompt instructions into these major categories:
  1. Display familiarity with a concept.
  2. Display familiarity with the relations between/among concepts.
  3. Display familiarity with a process.
  4. Display familiarity with argumentation.

may encounter. As they confront ambiguous verbs within their examination prompts, they should be encouraged to ask their instructors for clarification.

IDENTIFYING DISCIPLINE-SPECIFIC AND GENERAL ACADEMIC VOCABULARY

Vocabulary provides another important topic for student literacy research. When studying essay examination prompts, students can work in groups to identify those words in the prompts that may be central to the discipline. In Prompts 1 and 2, my students identified the geographical lexicon as *population, rate of growth, natural resource system, inhabitants, planet, illegal immigration, magnitude of the flows, migration,* and *immigration policy.* In Prompt 3, from biology, they identified *Kingdom Fungi, Divisions, members, symbioses,* and *organisms.* Discussions following this exercise focused on special meanings that ordinary words have within disciplines. (For example, what does "members" mean in biology texts?) Students can also discuss the possible relationships among the terms and concepts within a discipline, such as among *kingdom, divisions,* and *members.*

In addition to identifying the special vocabulary words from the disciplines, students can use these and other sample texts to examine a more inclusive lexicon, those words that tend to cross academic disciplines. As references for these exercises, they can consult the academic vocabulary lists provided by Nation (1990), Praninskas (1972), and others. My students put into the "general academic" category words and phrases within the prompts – such as *commanded attention, sound, grounded, justification* from Prompt 1; *stressing, adherents, imitations* from Prompt 2; *in regards to* [sic] and *encountered* in Prompt 3 – all of which might appear in texts from other disciplines. After the students listed the general academic words that they found in these examples, they were asked to categorize them according to their meanings or grammatical features.

It should be noted that the vocabulary exercises suggested here are considerably different from some that still appear in academic literacy textbooks. These exercises stress relationships among words and concepts within a discipline or a genre, and they help students to understand the functions that certain words, as concepts, can serve within larger disciplinary communities or within their DS classrooms.

EXPLORING RHETORICAL FEATURES

During their analyses, students discover that some prompts require them to take particular roles as writers ("citizen of the planet" or "policy analyst"); and even if the role is not stated, they may be expected to write like members of a disciplinary community, such as cultural geographers or biologists. Sometimes the audience ("government officials") and context are also specified. Occasionally, a genre is indicated by name[5] ("a plan of action"), but more frequently, students are given explicit instructions for organizing their responses. Thus, those features that are considered traditionally rhetorical (audience, purpose, role; see Coe, 1994) can be present in prompts from DS classrooms.

Throughout the discussion of research, the emphasis is on student discovery: of texts within a genre and of similarities and differences among conventions within these texts. While the students make these discoveries, they also discuss what they are required to do in their DS classrooms: their particular responsibilities to these texts. In general, their findings are similar to those of Horowitz, who concluded that "generally speaking, the academic writer's task is not to create personal meaning, but to find, organize and present data according to fairly explicit instructions" (1986a, p. 445).

Text-external research

The genre: An encyclopedia entry

Texts are not autonomous; they cannot be separated from roles, purposes, and contexts. Readers and writers of texts are influenced by their past educational experiences, by their experiences with the genre, by culture, by content, by context, and by many other factors. Before reading or writing a text, then, students should consider some of the factors that may influence their processing and comprehension. Though any genre exemplars can be used to begin an analysis, I have chosen encyclopedia entries because they are commonly consulted by students and they serve a variety of purposes in academic contexts. Not incidentally, these texts are often difficult for academics to write, because authors must boil down what they know about a subject into laypersons' language, assuming no special prior knowledge of the reader. Working in groups, my students answered these questions about several encyclopedia entries on the same subject.

1. What are these texts named? Are they organized in any particular way?
2. Who are the writers and readers? Why would someone write these texts? Why would you, or someone else, read them?
3. What is the context for writing these texts? (When and where were they published? By whom?)
4. What do these factors tell us about text biases or foci?

5 Seldom are students shown models of texts in a genre, however.

Why do we study the sociocultural issues that influence texts? One reason is that some students believe that most published texts are autonomous and impartial, that what is printed is "the truth." My novice students think of encyclopedia entries as particularly objective; "They just list the facts of the matter," according to one. To demonstrate text partiality, we need only compare the treatment of a topic in one encyclopedia entry with the treatment of the same topic produced for another context. For example, a Chinese colleague[6] and I compared for the students the presentations of a topic, "Otto von Bismarck," found in a recently published American encyclopedia and a Chinese volume published immediately after the Cultural Revolution (1978). Though the dates (birth, death, wars, and European conferences) were equivalent in the texts, the interpretations of this German diplomat and politician's life were considerably different. The Chinese interpretation was Marxist, discussing Bismarck's "exploitation of colonies" and his "hegemony." The American version reported Bismarck's feats as, for the most part, important and remarkable accomplishments. This comparison demonstrates that even writers of encyclopedias are influenced by their cultures, their text histories, and their schooling – not to mention the ideologies of the publishers.

By completing what is sometimes called "critical reading" (see Adams, 1989), in which the cultural, political, and esthetic biases of a text are examined, students discover that all texts are partial: Information is sometimes omitted, assertions are not supported, particular views of the world prevail. Developing hypotheses about who wrote the text, when and where, and for whom the texts are written are important if students are to process texts intelligently. It is also essential to compare texts from different contexts and cultures in order to grasp fully the nature of social construction.

Processing and strategies research

In reading

We also need to help students to study a variety of processing strategies that may be employed by readers, who are influenced by sociocultural factors. Processing a textbook assignment for a multiple-choice test should be different from processing it for an essay examination. Searching for specific terms or a single quotation within a reading require different strategies than attempting to understand text argumentation. Processing and comprehending a text with new, difficult information and vocabulary, particularly in a second or foreign language, is considerably different from processing something on a familiar topic in one's own

6 I would like to thank Professor Zhang Zheng-sheng for this contribution.

language. It can be useful for students to study how other readers process texts for different purposes as they assess their own task representation and text processing. On occasion, I have brought to the literacy classroom a more experienced student, preferably to discuss reading with which the literacy students are familiar, such as assignments from a class they are all attending. Here are some of the questions that can be posed to this expert student.

1. What are your goals for reading this text? (Or) What have you been asked to do with this text?
2. How does reading this text differ from reading other materials assigned in classes? Why?
3. What specific strategies do you use? Do you skim first for headings and italicized words? Do you pause to take notes? Where? Why? Do you mark the text? With questions? Comments? Do you read aloud? Why? Do you use a dictionary to look up words, or do you skip over one you don't know? Which words do you look up, and why?

For most of these processing questions, I am indebted to a volume on reading by Davies (1995, pp. 52–53), who suggests that research into reading strategies can be organized into a number of categories: control of reading process (rate, marking text, etc.), monitoring reading (making predictions, forming hypotheses, referring to task), utilizing background knowledge (of similar texts, of cultural and personal experience, of knowledge, of format), interacting with the text (questioning, translating, expressing feelings), and utilizing the text itself (examining genre, register style, context, clause structure, vocabulary).

With this processing research should come analysis and reflection. For example, students can write up what they have discovered about expert text processing using the answers from their interview questions. However, they should reflect upon their own experiences with processing as well. When my literacy students who were enrolled in a history class were assigned a novel entitled *1492*, by Homer Aridjis, they had considerable difficulty understanding its purposes for this class. So I asked them to write a letter to a friend, explaining what the book was about and the difficulties they were facing in processing and comprehending it. Here is an example:

Dear Jorge,

In my history class we are reading *1492*. This book is pretty good in the way that it takes a look at things through a peasant point of view. On the other hand, this book is kind of hard to understand because it uses a lot of words I've never had to read before. So I spent a lot of time just looking up words.

Best, Max

When they had finished their letters, I asked the students to speculate about why the novel had been assigned for a history class. Then, together, we developed questions about purposes and text processing that they could ask of the DS instructor who had assigned the reading.

What is being suggested here is that processing of readings can, and should, vary depending on a number of sociocultural, textual, and personal factors. There is no one reading process; rather, there are multiple strategies for accessing texts. If students conduct research and reflect upon these factors in our classrooms and develop a repertoire of their own processing strategies, they will be able to face future reading tasks with more confidence.

In writing

As in the case of reading, strategies for completing writing assignments can, and should, vary considerably. Stanley Fish (1985, p. 438) notes that all linguistic knowledge (including literacies) is "dynamic rather than invariant," and we should keep this in mind when we ask students to research their approaches to situated writing tasks. Again, we need to encourage students to consider sociocultural as well as textual and personal factors: the variety of issues that influence what happens in the production of a specific text. We can also ask students to reflect upon their goals for writing and their strategies for accomplishing a task. I pose questions such as the following: "How do you prepare to write? Where and when do you write? How do you encourage your own fluency and editing?" This is one student's [uncorrected] response to these questions about her own writing processes:

When I sit down to write, I usually think of what I was going to write about first. After I have figure it out in my mined, then I start writing it out. but as I write along, I would still continuing thinking of what I'm going to write about, and sometime I would express my thought out loud as though I was talking with someone. I would usually write most of my writing assignment on my table in my bedroom. Most of my writing would be in the early morning around four o'clock, where everybody in my family was still sleeping and my room would be very quiet.

In addition to considering their typical preparations for writing, students need to think about how their goals, processes, and strategies may vary, depending on the task and the rhetorical situation. They also need to consider the nature of the task, particularly as it relates to other assignments in the course. Here are some of the questions that students might ask to research a specific writing assignment, with some added commentary on each topic.

1. *About the prompt:* How is this assignment written? Is the problem stated? Is the viewpoint of the instructor clear? What are the specific instructions for

text organization, for context, and for reader and writer roles? What topics are most important to address? How can I get clarification for those things about the assignment that I don't understand?

Commentary: Students should be encouraged to go to the source – the faculty member who made the assignment – but only after they have done their best to deconstruct the prompt and formulate questions. DS faculty do not like to be asked, "What do you want?" particularly if the student is uninformed. However, they are often quite open to students who have thought about the assignment and can ask specific questions.

2. *Criteria for evaluation:* How will the responses be evaluated? Will instructors weight the grades for content, organization, argumentation, or editing? Or will the instructor grade holistically? How can we find out more about evaluation criteria?

Commentary: One of the most frustrating experiences for students is not understanding what will be considered important in an assignment. Some faculty are open to discussing evaluation criteria, and some even distribute criteria sheets. However, others are quite closed about how they (or their teaching assistants) grade, fearing that if they say too much, they will give students an unfair advantage. This is a strange attitude, but it is remarkably prevalent among DS faculty.

There are more subtle ways of discovering grading criteria, however. If the assignment is an important one, students can draft a version and take it to the faculty member for comment. Often, the faculty are pleased that students have written a draft in advance, and they help them with their revisions. As faculty provide assistance, the implicit criteria for evaluation become clear.

3. *Classroom context:* What do I know about this particular class for which I am writing the assignment? What do I know about the values of the professor and of his or her discipline? About the important arguments or concepts in the course? About the influential readings?

Commentary: These questions provide useful opportunities for students to review their notes and assigned readings and to talk with other students about the particular "take" on the discipline that this faculty member has. There always seem to be a few students who are particularly savvy; these students can be consulted about what is expected.

4. *Past experiences:* Have I ever written something that is similar to this assignment in my first or second language? What strategies did I use to complete the assignment? Were they successful? Why or why not? How should they be modified for this assignment?

Commentary: A written reflection is one way for students to approach this research. In one case, when students were in the process of writing a research paper, I asked them to compose a short reflection answering these questions: "Have you ever conducted research before? What were you asked to do? What kind of paper did you write?" Here is one of my student's responses:

I have only had one experience with research. It was in my junior year in high school. What the teacher made us do was first we had to get a map, next we were supposed to mark a trail from Los Angeles to New York. While we made our trail we had to mark places we would like to visit. For each one of the places we selected we had to write a one page research paper which included famous sites, national parks, agriculture or whatever we thought was important. Our teacher gave us one week to finish the whole assignment. For the next five days, I spent most of my time in a library writing things about places I had never heard of. But what I liked was I learn a lot about these places and others that I read about by mistake.

Another student had this to say about his past term-paper experiences:

The kind of papers that I did before were not so long as to call them term papers. During my high school years, my English teachers were the ones who made me do essays (5 paragraphs). It didn't matter how long as long as it had the information they wanted. In my government class my teacher just told us once to write one page per person for our group. It might be called a term paper, but I don't think it would be cause it's just talking about someone who was dead a long time ago. Many of my friends had term papers but always had trouble turning them in on time. I know that I'm going to have a lot more papers in university, but I just have to try to use my time wisely and work hard.

Once the students had written their reflections about previous experiences, we talked about the strategies they had used in the past, and then added to these strategies as we discussed the current assignment.

5. *Establishing an approach:* How am I going to approach this particular assignment? How will I choose the topic? Can I negotiate the assignment so that it is more to my liking?

Commentary: We need to do more in our literacy classes concerning negotiation or variation, approaches that make the assignment more personally interesting. In a study of students' writing strategies as they approached academic tasks, Leki (1995) found that some could manipulate or resist the various assignments given to them, often quite successfully. For example, some students related everything they wrote (or read) to what they knew. A Chinese student brought her language and home-country experience into every assignment, therefore making it more familiar and manageable. Like this student, a Laotian student whom I interviewed spent considerable time negotiating with faculty members so that she could use her past experiences or incorporate material from her previous papers into her new texts (Johns, 1992). Other students choose not to write to the assignment. Leki speaks of a French student who was assigned a term paper in which she was to discuss how Southern women in the United States were portrayed in novels from the 1950s (1995, p. 243):

> When she read the novel, [Julie] found herself interested in only one of the women and wrote only about this one despite the directions to consider all women. Although she expressed some concern about her choice, she nevertheless stayed with her decision . . . not following the teachers' directions to consider all women in the novel but instead rewriting the terms of the assignment to suit what she thought she could do best. Her grade for the paper was an A.

It must be noted, however, that "each example of resistance, was, at least in part, based upon reasonable principle" (Leki, 1995, p. 251). Students have to be wise about what ways they can successfully negotiate and resist. One of my students attempted to use the data for a high school paper on gangs for his university Western Civilization paper ("I got an A once; maybe I can get one again."), but his instructor would not hear of it.

6. *Setting goals:* How much time do I have to spend on this assignment? Where will I start? What steps will I take? What will I do if I become discouraged, confused, or frustrated? How many drafts of the assignment will I write? Whom will I consult about the drafts?

Commentary: Most successful students set goals in advance and work on their assignments over time. Students not only need to plan times during which they will work on assignments, they need to decide how much of their time they are going to invest and in what way. For some students, writing is unfamiliar and difficult, and they require considerable time and support to get a satisfactory grade. For others, writing is much easier and even enjoyable; thus, there can be less long-term investment.

The purposes for this student research and reflection are several: to encourage an understanding of text histories so that students can draw from previous experiences; to discuss the particular demands of an assignment, specifically, how it is different or similar to previously assigned tasks; and to understand that goals and processes may differ depending on the task itself, the task evaluator, individual motivation, text and schooling histories, and many other factors. There is no one reading or writing process, as we know; rather, there are many. Just as each text and task is situated and somewhat different, so, too, should each reading or writing process differ from others.

In this section, I have discussed student research into and reflection on tasks and text processing. In this effort, I must acknowledge a debt to the Process Movement and Psycholinguistic-Cognitive theories of literacy, those views that brought metacognition, metalanguage, strategies, and the study of reading and writing processes into literacy teaching. At the same time, I suggest that our literacy classes go beyond students' problem solving and processes to the context, linking "process" with "how writing works in the world" (Giroux, 1983). In this way, students can develop an understanding that task planning and processes depend not only on themselves but also on many historical and current social influences.

Research beyond the classroom

Interviews with discipline-specific faculty and expert students

Much student research on texts and processes can be completed in literacy classrooms, but students also need to go outside: to observe, to question, and to develop hypotheses. One productive way for students to test their hypotheses about texts, roles, and contexts, and about writers' and readers' purposes, is to interview DS faculty members. In preparing their interview questions, students must first ask themselves what their purposes are. Do they want to find out about a specific class and the nature of the assignments? Do they want to ask questions about specialist text form and content, about vocabulary and argumentation? Do they want to hear about the socioliterate practices of the instructor: his or her discipline and disciplinary practices, favorite classes, and requirements? Sometimes the students are interested in several of these general topics;[7] however, I encourage them to focus on one topic and to pursue it in depth during the interview.

Each group of four or five students decides on a topic, then the groups begin to develop a series of questions to pose to the faculty expert. They share their questions with other student groups as they work on refining them. In some cases, the students conduct a practice interview with their literacy teacher or a student volunteer before the DS faculty interview takes place, in order to reduce the possibility for misunderstanding or insult and to ensure that the information desired will be elicited by the questions posed. These activities provide excellent opportunities for rehearsing question posing, a skill that is both necessary and difficult for many students (McKenna, 1987). When practicing the interviews, students can work on pronunciation, intonation, vocabulary choice, and pragmatic considerations such as topic nomination and turn taking. As the students practice, the literacy teacher acts as informant and facilitator, providing commentary and critique when necessary.

When the students are ready to conduct their interviews, each group visits the faculty member.[8] In most cases, the roles are planned: Certain

7 There are also some students, of course, who are interested in none. However, I provide incentives, such as points.
8 We sometimes invite faculty to our literacy classes for these discussions as well.

students ask the questions, others take notes, and others tape record (if permitted). After the interviews, the group meets to write up their findings for a report to their literacy class.

DISCIPLINARY PRACTICES INTERVIEWS

The possibilities for interview topics relating to texts, tasks, and other classroom issues are many. One example that focuses on the faculty member's professional interests as they relate to his disciplinary community is provided here. These are the questions the students prepared.

1. Why did you study this subject (e.g., biology)?
2. What is your educational background? Why did you choose to complete your degrees at the educational institutions you attended?
3. When did you complete your thesis or dissertation? What was the title? (And sometimes: What does the title mean?) May we see a copy? What methodology did you use? Is this a common methodology in your discipline? Have you published something from your dissertation? May we see a copy?
4. Are you still interested in your dissertation topic, or are you now involved in other research topics?
5. How do you use your dissertation or current research in teaching your classes, if at all? Which classes are most related to your research interests and dissertation topic? Why?
6. Are any of your students doing research with you? What are their roles in the research process? Do they co-author the papers?
7. Would you encourage today's students to pursue your research interests? Why or why not?
8. What are the important research or teaching topics in your discipline today? How can we find out about them?

Using their notes and their recordings, the student groups wrote up their interview results as a brief research report, citing as sources quotations from the faculty member as well as elements from the dissertation or class textbooks. It should be noted that a dissertation itself can provide a number of possibilities for student research: They can discuss who reads it (the "committee"), how it is structured, the content and form of the hypotheses, data collection, and the use of nonlinear information such as formulas, charts, and graphs. This student exposure to disciplinary rather than pedagogical texts and experiences can lead to useful discussions and discoveries.

Emboldened by their interview successes, students often approach other faculty to conduct similar, less formal discussions, and, not incidentally, ask specific questions about their own future study and involvement in a disciplinary community.

TEXT-AS-ARTIFACTS INTERVIEWS

Other students are more concerned about their current literacies than they are about the rules and practices of a disciplinary community. In these cases, another type of scripted interview, about pedagogical artifacts, can take place. As has been noted, the textbook is the most typical classroom reading for many undergraduates, and for some graduate students as well; thus these can be chosen as artifacts for interviews.

The following set of interview questions were posed to a faculty member in his office by four members of my literacy class.

1. Why was X textbook chosen for X class? Was it chosen by you? If so, why do you prefer it to the other textbooks available? Was it chosen by another member of the faculty or a department committee? What were the reasons for their choice?
2. What do you see as the function of the textbook in the class? Is it a reference? Does it provide the most important reading?
3. What particular aids in the textbook are most important for student use in this class? Why? How do they relate to the classroom goals?
4. What are the central concepts, topics, or ideas for the classroom that this textbook includes? What parts of the textbook are not as important for the course? Why?
5. How would you read or study for this class, using this textbook? (Students may assist the faculty member in this discussion by turning to a chapter and asking the faculty member to show how she or he would approach the reading and study of the text.) Would you take notes, gloss the margins, or use another method? What would you take notes on? Why would you study in this way?
6. Do you read textbooks to keep up with your discipline?[9] If not, what do you read? How does what you read as a professional differ from a textbook reading? (And, for the braver students: Why don't students read the kinds of texts you read?)

Students find this kind of interview useful, even if they are not enrolled in the faculty member's class. It helps them to understand the textbook as genre and to see its potential relationships to classroom practices. In some cases, students find that faculty have not thought much about their textbooks, and this can be frustrating or revealing. In other cases, the faculty turn the tables: They ask students to talk about the textbooks and how the students read them. Whatever happens, these sessions can become learning experiences for all concerned.

9 I had assumed that DS faculty do not read textbooks. This is not always the case. One instructor told me that if he is looking into an aspect of his discipline with which he is unfamiliar, he might turn to a textbook in this area.

Participant observation

Our students are, and will continue to be, participants in academic endeavors. Another research goal, then, is to convert them from students into participant observers, to change what is often a passive role into an active one. What does this mean for the student researchers? Doheny-Farina and Odell (1985, p. 508) describe participant observation in the following manner:

> . . . the researchers must adopt a dual role – that of both participant and observer. As participants, researchers try to develop an empathetic relationship with the individuals they are studying. Researchers must try to see things from these individuals' point of view, becoming – at last vicariously – participants in the life of the group to which the individuals belong. Researchers, however, must also be able to distance themselves, to look at phenomena from an outsider's point of view.

For students, this juxtaposition of participant in academic classrooms and observer (budding researcher) is ideal. It enables them to participate fully, yet it requires them to attempt to "see things from [the faculty or expert student] point of view."

The following features of participant observation, adapted from a discussion by Spindler (1982), can be applied to the roles that students take as researchers:

1. Observation is contextualized: The significance of events is seen in the framework of the immediate setting. [Students observe and participate in a class or a lecture. They observe the elements of a rhetorical situation in which discourses serve important purposes.]
2. If possible, observation is prolonged and repetitive. Students should have more than one experience with a classroom culture in order to pose hypotheses. [If enrolled in a class, they attend class regularly; they are able to make prolonged and repetitive observations that assist them in recording what they see and making hypotheses about the meanings embedded in the situation. Though repeated observation is not always possible, one participant observer experience can still be valuable to students and literacy class discussion.]
3. Hypotheses and questions emerge as the researcher observes a specific setting. [Students begin to develop hypotheses not only about the classroom or other academic cultures, but about texts and other discourses and their own evolving literacies.]
4. Researchers make inferences about the "native" [faculty or disciplinary community] view of reality. [These can be inferences about a faculty member's discipline and research, goals and objectives for the content class, about testing, or about ways of grading.]

5. Student researchers make observations about their own emerging literacy practices. [This element was added to the Spindler list, because it is valuable for developing metacognitive awareness of reading and writing processes and for approaching the challenges of future literacy tasks and situations.]

Of course, our students can only be novice participant observers. Most will never qualify as full-blown educational ethnographers. However, encouraging them to both observe and record what they see is enabling as they begin to understand the relationships between their literacy experiences and the contexts they are observing.

IN ONE CLASSROOM: USING LITERACY JOURNALS

In several of my classes, students have written literacy journals, not as personal responses for writing, but as participant observer records. In some ways, these journals are typical of literacy journals in that students are encouraged to employ their "own style and voice" (Fulweiler, 1982) and to explore possibilities without being corrected either by their fellow students or by their instructor. However, these tools are also different from personal, Expressivist journals found in many classes, in that they are devoted to recording and analyzing the interactions in spoken and written discourses and the various roles people and texts play within academic contexts.[10]

When the journals were assigned in one literacy class, I introduced some principles of participant observation to the students. Initially, I asked them to apply these principles as they wrote about their own literacy class. In weekly, one-page journal entries, they jotted down observations and developed hypotheses about my (implicit) goals and values and the purposes for the tasks assigned, thus developing a concept of the classroom culture from the instructor's view.[11] They also were asked to analyze, with empathy, the cultures of their cooperative learning groups within the class: the values and motivations of the various group members, the group interactions, responses to literacy practices of other members of the group, and peer editing interactions. As they wrote, the students developed hypotheses and metalanguage about the class cultures as well as about their own goals and literacy practices. They shared some of their weekly journal entries with their groups and with the entire class. As the term progressed, the hypotheses became more focused. For example, the students hypothesized that I was more interested in academic writing

10 For a more complete discussion of these journals, see my chapter entitled "Coherence as a Cultural Phenomenon: Employing Ethnographic Principles in the Academic Milieu," in Connor and Johns (1990b).
11 The results of these observations are fascinating: Our goals and tasks are often seen in very different ways by our students.

than personal writing ("So much argumentation!"), and that the chief reasons for cooperative learning sessions were to solve literacy problems and peer-review papers. They also developed hypotheses about their fellow students' previous literacy practices and theories of reading and writing, attempting to take an academic perspective. The journals became the focus of class discussions and were important to developing improved group interaction, as well as raising the level of understanding of particular, contextualized literacy practices.

However, when the students were asked to examine the DS class in which they were enrolled, they became frustrated, because there was so much happening that they did not know what to observe and record. They complained that they "just could not put it all down." In participant observer situations, ethnographers attempt "thick description" (Ibrahim, 1993), recording everything they see and experience, but this approach appears to be difficult – if not impossible – for many literacy students. Thus I decided to modify the rules for participant observation to be more appropriate to my students' abilities. I suggested single topics for observation journal entries in their DS class, and I provided focused questions for these topics. Later in the term, no question proposing was necessary, because students began to select their own topics for research.

The discussion that follows is based on the semester in which my students were enrolled in a world history class (Johns, 1990b). The first topic I proposed for their participant observation journals was the professor himself. I asked: What is he like? What does he expect? One student wrote the following on the subject:

Joe [the professor told students that he wanted to be addressed by his first name] expect the class to be pretty much on time and present on the days of class. He also think that notes should be taken and that your attention will be on him during the lectures. He will tolerate drinking soft drinks in class as long as your careful not to tip over the glass and that it is not played with during discussions.

The next set of journal assignments was devoted to topics central to class lecture and discussion. Students were asked to respond to one or several of these questions: "Which topics are emphasized in this course? How are they related to each other? How are they dealt with in the lectures?" One student, who was having great difficulty keeping up with the class, made the following comment about the class topics and the way they were approached by the professor:

I don't understand his class very well. He sometimes confuse about historical facts. He also jump from one event to another without even stopping to see if we have any question.

Later in the term, when the journal responses became unscripted and the students chose their own topics, they often commented about themselves as participants in this class culture: about their responses to assignments and essays and their own efforts to perform the tasks assigned. Rather than continue to study the class culture, they were anxious to analyze their own literacy practices in this academic context. Here is one personal literacy response from a journal after an examination was returned:

> After looking over my paper, I discovered that I need to spend more time in analyzing the question being asked. When I write my papers, I tend to touch around the question, without answering directly. This is an extremely bad quality, for on an exam the teacher is going to want to focus on the main idea of the paper.

Throughout this semester, the observation journals were important elements in our literacy class. They led not only to useful class discussions, but to further research in the form of expert student and DS faculty interviews and the collection of artifacts. Each week, a few students volunteered to share their journal entries, reading them aloud to their groups or to the class as a whole.

As the students were practicing participant observation in our literacy class, there had been considerable comment on how reading and writing tasks should be approached, on what instructor goals for students might be, and on the effective and ineffective practices in their group work. When the students began to observe the DS class, the topics sometimes shifted, but the literacy class discussion that resulted was fully as important to their practices and understandings.

ALTERNATIVE PARTICIPANT OBSERVATION RESEARCH

Participant observation can take place in many contexts. A teacher might ask students to record and participant-observe an academic lecture on a campus, requiring them to hypothesize, from a single instance, some of the "native" views of a particular academic culture. In one such attempt, I sent students to a public academic lecture on a familiar topic, given in a large auditorium. Rather than requiring an open-ended journal response, which would probably have resulted in attempts at word-by-word note taking, I asked the students to listen for two things: the question the lecturer had posed in his research, and the types of data he had analyzed to answer the question. I wanted the students to leave the lecture with the understanding that in most academic communities, problems or questions are posed and data are collected and analyzed to answer these questions, though question type and data collected may vary according to discipline. My students attempted to respond to my assignment, but they had difficulty sorting through the detail and vocabulary of the lecture to find the research question. I assured the students that they were not alone in their difficulties, and I shared with them an article by Arden-Close

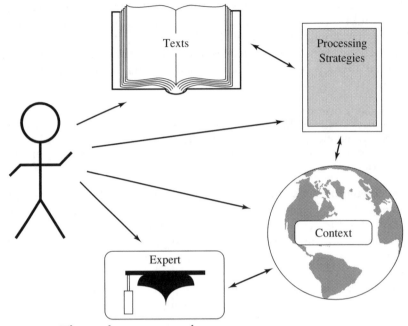

Figure 1   The student as researcher.

(1993), who discusses the complicated relationship between vocabulary and argumentation in academic lectures. This led to a discussion about the words and phrases that students could listen for to assist them in finding the key points in a lecture (see Olsen & Huckin, 1990). It can be seen, then, that in their attempt to discover the argumentation within a lecture, students also discovered some of their own difficulties with academic listening comprehension. From their concerns, we built a lesson based on listening and note taking.

Another assignment involves student visitation of a lecture or lab for a class in which they plan to enroll. In this case, a "thick description" of everything they observe may be useful. Here is one assignment I have given:

Visit a lecture class or a laboratory section. Record everything you see and experience: whether and how students pay attention, take notes, and ask questions; the organization and style of the lab or lecture; how and when the readings for the class are mentioned and anything else that you find interesting.

These student observations, recorded in their observation journals, can be augmented by a short interview with a member of the class, the faculty member, or the lab instructor to get a "native" perspective on what is observed. For other assignments, students can participant-observe in the library or at a meeting of one of the campus student organizations. Whatever the locale, the purposes are to encourage the development of a more detached stance about activities in a context, a metalanguage about a culture, and a more critical awareness of texts, roles, and contexts.

This chapter has suggested some of the ways in which students can research texts, roles, and contexts and their own strategies for completing tasks, and those of others, in order to gain a better understanding of situated socioliterate practices. Figure 1 illustrates some of the topics and research foci with which students can be involved.

Students need to develop a sense of the complexities of literacy practices: that texts are varied and influenced by many factors, that text processing will change for a number of reasons, that assignments can be negotiated and even resisted, and that many faculty are approachable. We practitioners strive to prepare students for lifelong literacy. Student research projects, such as those described here, provide some of the most important ways to effect this preparation.

7 *The socioliterate classroom*
Basic tenets and goals

When students from [diverse] backgrounds experiment with academic
discourse, they are doing more than trying on a linguistic disguise; they are
experimenting as well with new identities, new ways of thinking and
being. . . . Increasingly, theorists and researchers acknowledge that the
linguistic challenges these students face are intricately connected to a broad
web of cognitive, social and affective concerns . . . that these students navigate
not only among ways of using language but, indeed, among worlds (DiPardo,
1993, p. 7).

After fourteen years of being taught that the text has all the answers, is it any
surprise that some students find it hard to understand that they must read
rhetorically, they must ask about author's purpose and context in order to use
knowledge productively (Geisler, 1994, p. 49)?

At some point in their professional lives, most literacy instructors must
have asked themselves a question similar to this one:

Given the short time I have to work with my students, how can I best prepare
them for the varied and unpredictable literacy challenges that they will
confront in their academic and professional lives?

No matter how ideal or constrained our teaching environments, we
always seem to have too little time in our classes to accomplish what
appears to be the impossible: equipping students with the confidence,
motivation, language, skills, abilities, and insights necessary to succeed in
textual worlds that we, and they, cannot predict. This chapter suggests
some general tenets and pedagogical principles that can assist us in answering the vexing question posed above. The chapter also presents specific ways in which these tenets and principles can be carried out.
  The following questions will be addressed:

1. What should be the basic tenets of a socioliterate pedagogy? What
   general guidelines for resource exploitation, reading text selection,
   and approaches to writing should be applied?
2. What goals can be established to prepare students to analyze, comprehend, process, and reflect while navigating future textual worlds?

  Before beginning this discussion, I must acknowledge that there are
many literacy teaching contexts for which the examinations and curric-

114

ula are established or the classes are very large. In these contexts, practitioners are often bound by strict administrative constraints and by unsurmountable enrollment exigencies. I have taught students and conducted seminars with teachers in these environments, and I am well aware of the frustrations induced among creative and responsible practitioners. However, I am always surprised by what still can be done: what thoughtful teachers can still insert into discussion, into reading, and into writing, despite the pressures of the teaching situation. Much of what I suggest can be accomplished if the only text available is the textbook, as the practitioners with whom we worked in China in the 1980s demonstrated (see Brosnahan et al., 1987). Much can be accomplished even if classes are large and examinations are set by the administration.

What I suggest here can be carried out, in some form, in every pedagogical context. The only requirement is an imaginative literacy teacher.

Basic tenets

The basic tenets of a socioliterate classroom have been introduced in various ways in previous chapters. They will be summarized here and a few possibilities for their realization in classroom practice will be suggested.

Draw from all possible resources

Chapters 5 and 6 outlined some of the many ways in which we literacy practitioners, and our students, can act as mediators and researchers within our campus contexts. In these roles, we need to visit, observe, interview, and reflect upon rhetorical contexts outside our own classrooms in order to be introduced to, and perhaps influence, academic socioliterate practices.

INTERVIEW FACULTY

We can also invite experts to our classrooms. Discipline-specific or fellow literacy faculty can be invited to provide information and insights on a particular topic. After the United Nations Conference on Women held in China (1995), for example, I asked a Chinese-speaking professor who had participated in the conference to come to class and discuss her experiences with my literacy students. Because an editorial would be assigned to the students after the talk, the students worked in groups before the speaker arrived to plan a series of questions that would encourage her to express her personal views. After the professor had left, the students were given a number of editorials to analyze for genre features, and then they produced their own texts, many of which were from the vantage point of the faculty speaker.[1]

Faculty can also be invited to speak about student work. They can be asked to talk about the kinds of assignments they give and ways in which grades are allocated. They can be encouraged to bring to class examples of good (and bad) papers written in response to specific assignments. Another possibility is to ask faculty to discuss the reading assignments in their classes: how they expect students to approach texts, and what they want students to learn from assigned reading. Sometimes, if faculty require several types of reading, they can be asked to discuss the purposes that each of the readings serves in their classes. Faculty who have consciously encouraged critical thinking in their classes can be invited to give examples of the types of thinking required in their disciplines.

INTERVIEW EXPERIENCED STUDENTS

There are also advantages to asking experienced students to visit our classes. Some of our most successful presentations have been by students who were previously enrolled in our literacy classes and are now more advanced and doing well. These students often have different perspectives from faculty: about assignments, about literacy challenges and frustrations, about coping with work overload, and about texts and academic contexts. Some more advanced students are very effective in discussing the nature of compulsory examinations and their successful and unsuccessful attempts to prepare for them. Another topic that expert students can discuss is their strategies for completing literacy tasks effectively. As Leki (1995) has pointed out, students develop a variety of approaches for achieving their ends, including consulting other students and modifying their assignments to fit their personal goals and purposes. Visits from successful (or initially unsuccessful) advanced students provide an effective wake-up call for currently enrolled students, who may have underestimated literacy tasks, or conversely, may be frightened by the challenges they will face in the future.

INTERVIEW STAFF AND OTHER PROFESSIONALS

In addition to students and faculty, many other people can be invited to our classes. Literacy students benefit from hearing personnel involved in financial aid or career planning, from doctors in the health services unit or high-level administrators. Students can also benefit from listening to people from the community, particularly those who are in the professions

---

1 They even included the short biographical note that generally accompanies signed editorials: "XXX was born and educated in Taiwan and is now an Assistant Dean at San Diego State University. She represented XXX, a Non-governmental Organization (NGO), at the conference.

to which the students aspire. Our university alumni office and campus departments have given us the names of professionals who are graduates; no doubt most institutions have some type of graduate and professional network.

Especially in EFL contexts, it is important for students to hear various native speakers of English so that they can become familiar with colloquial speech and dialectal variation. We can invite to class someone who can talk about a topic of interest to our students. While I was teaching in China, I invited my 16-year-old daughter to speak about "teenage hooligans" in America and their discourses, a topic of great interest to my students. In Morocco, my colleagues and I invited a French-English bilingual agronomist to speak on genres in the two languages. Other EFL colleagues have invited businesspeople, librarians, tourists, and visiting faculty to address literacy classes.

Before the speaker appears, students should prepare for the visit in some way: by writing questions, by predicting what the speaker will discuss, or by reading an article of interest to, or written by, the speaker. After the speaker has presented to the students, there should be a post-talk follow-up. Students can discuss major points the speaker made and then summarize these points in writing, or they can reflect upon what they learned about a particular topic or strategy. Students can also be asked to write to the speaker. My students have written both memos and letters to those who have spoken in the class, assignments that provide opportunities for students to produce texts from a genre addressed to real audiences outside the classroom. Since audience is crucial to these assignments, we spend considerable prewriting time dealing with questions such as: "What kind of person is this speaker? What would he or she like to hear from us about the presentation? What values or interests does he or she appear to have? How can we appropriately thank the speaker for taking the time to visit? How should the text be organized? Should we send copies of the memos to anyone else, such as the speaker's supervisor?" Sometimes each of the students writes a separate memo or letter to the speaker; on other occasions we cooperate in writing a single text.

In addition to exposing students in an organized way to the textual worlds outside the classroom, it is also important to bring the world to the students in the form of reading and writing experiences. Therefore, the next two sections deal with issues of reading text selection and reading-writing assignments.

Select reading texts carefully

As I noted earlier, not all suggestions made here can be realized in every literacy context. However, many can, and I urge readers to consider what may be possible for them. Following are the suggested criteria for text selection in many literacy classes.

FOR AUTHENTICITY AND COMPLETENESS

As we know, we cannot re-create a large variety of rhetorical contexts in our classrooms. Nor can we duplicate some of the reader and writer roles that students will be expected to take in the future. However, we can expose students to authentic texts, "(those) generated outside of, and for purposes separate to, the requirements of English language teaching" (Arnold, 1991, p. 237). If at all possible, these texts should not be simplified. Researchers have found that good simplification of texts, which retains all major text features, is very difficult and seldom accomplished (Lautamatti, 1987; Montford, 1975). Nor should texts be written by practitioners especially for the classroom, a common practice when the curricula focus on specific grammar or vocabulary. Teacher-constructed readings are often even more artificial than simplified ones, distancing students from the important social forces that are brought to bear upon authentic discourses. After a study of teacher-constructed texts, Harste (1990) referred to them as "textoids . . . short texts that have nothing to do with the students' daily lives" (quoted in Bintz and Harste, 1991, p. 238).

The texts we choose should be full and unabridged, preserved just as they have been written, with letterheads, headings, spacing, fonts, visual detail, errors, and, if possible, even the quality and color of the paper. All of these features, and more, contribute to a text as genre exemplar and to the understanding of a genre by experienced readers and writers. Some literacy textbook writers replicate authentic discourses but strip them of all of these trappings and reprint only the corrected text for students. This is unfortunate, for much is lost.

FOR TEACHABILITY AND APPROPRIATENESS

As we select our texts, we should ask ourselves questions about their classroom exploitability: "Is the genre appropriate? Are the content, form, and argumentation suitable for our students' needs? Can we use this text for the activities we want to assign? What kinds of group work can arise from the use of the text? Can the text promote analysis and research using expert students and faculty? Is it significantly different from the other texts chosen so that an understanding of variety among texts can be gained? Can it become a model for speaking, reading, or writing? Can the text be used in some way to assist students to prepare for compulsory examinations?" These and other questions appropriate to our own teaching contexts should be posed as we make our decisions about text selection.

FOR SPECIFIC TEXT-EXTERNAL FACTORS

We also need to consider factors that are not within the texts themselves but that still contribute to genre knowledge. We may want to select texts that display varying writer roles and purposes, for example. For some literacy classes, such as theme-based (see Chapter 5), we can select texts that deal with a single topic as explored by a number of writers. For example, one of the selected texts can be written by an authority on the topic, another can be a student research paper, a third can be by someone who disagrees with the authority, and so on.

It is also important for students to study texts written for different audiences. They can be exposed to texts written for general audiences, such as articles from a news magazine. They can compare these readings for content, form, visual elements, and other features with texts on the same topic written in professional journals or in magazines for educated laypeople, such as *Scientific American*. With a consideration of audience comes the issue of community, for community members often write to familiar audiences, therefore making assumptions about what is known, what is valued, and how a text should be organized. DS community-insider assumptions are found, for example, in the text in which Watson and Crick reported their discovery of DNA. Arrington and Rose (1987, p. 308) tell us that

. . . the[se] authors needed to offer no elaborate explanations of what DNA is or why its structure should be "of considerable biological interest." They assumed readers already knew about their subject and would accept its inherent interest as a focus. They also assumed readers would accept their method of gathering and selecting evidence, testing it, judging its accuracy, with nature's structure as an overriding criterion.

In order to expose my students to community-specific academic texts, I have given them historiography articles written by and for historians or anthropology monographs written by and for anthropologists, texts from DS genres we have collected from their DS classes or during faculty interviews. As students read these texts, we talk about particular features that identify the discourse as having been written for community insiders: topics about which there appears to be disagreement within the community, methods of argumentation and use of data, politeness strategies, use of citation, text macrostructure, syntax, and morphology. I become acutely aware of how "insider" these texts are when my students begin asking "What's going on here?" as they read. When this happens, the students are asked to read aloud sections that are mysterious, those that are written by, and for, a disciplinary community. Then we attempt to determine what is going on by analyzing aspects of the discourse or interviewing faculty informants.

Related text-external factors that can affect reading text selection are context and mode. Students can examine texts that were originally spoken to specific audiences or texts that were originally written, such as letters to the editor. They can examine written texts from the same genre, such as editorials, appearing in the publications of different communities. One of my colleagues asks his students to bring to the class magazines of interest to them; then each student is asked to identify the various genres within the magazine, select one text, and analyze it for "insider" content, organization, vocabulary, visuals, and other features. Other students can be asked to bring texts from their first languages, written in their home communities or educational institutions.

FOR VISUALS AND OTHER TEXT-INTERNAL FEATURES

In addition to the text-external factors, we need to consider the text-internal elements that affect genre knowledge. Many texts include meta-messages, those features that are not part of the language itself but are essential for expert text processing and comprehension (see Enkvist, 1990). For some texts, pictures are included to enhance understanding. In others, such as science and technology discourses, nonlinguistic elements such as graphs, formulas, and charts may be central to the argumentation or explanation. There may also be formatting, design, text organization, or other features that give important metamessages, a notion that was mentioned when discussing wedding invitations in Chapter 3, but one that is also relevant to letters, flyers, memos, and many other genres.

What language-related text-internal factors might we consider in text selection? In one of his articles on contrastive rhetoric, Hinds (1987) argues that expository texts written by native-speakers of English are "writer-responsible": The writer must take responsibility for leading readers through the text. He contrasts heterogeneous writer-responsible, English-language cultures with "reader-responsible" ones, such as Japan, where a more homogeneous culture enables a writer to assume reader prior knowledge of form, content, values, and other generic features and thus may be less explicit. What are some of the writer-responsible features that assist readers to wend their way successfully through (expository) English discourses? A few of the most important are discussed below.

Early in their texts, writers often prereveal information about textual content, organization, and argumentation. A good thesis in an essay is a prerevealing move, for example. Here is one of the initial paragraphs of a book chapter on literacy, in which prerevealing takes place (Calfee, 1994, p. 19):

In this chapter I argue that although U.S. schools are meeting our children's academic and social needs today as well as they have in the past, the education agenda has undergone a fundamental transformation. I describe a program for curricular reform in literacy instruction that, unlike other contemporary alarms, starts with the schools as they are, and builds on the simplest of activities – the daily reading-writing lesson – to achieve fundamental change in schooling in the elementary grades. My argument rests on two propositions:

- *Critical literacy,* the literate use of language to problem solve and communicate, should be the primary aim of the elementary years of schooling.
- *The school as a community of inquiry,* a professional collective in which problem solving and communication are the norms, should be the aid of restructuring efforts.

My thesis is that these propositions are actually two sides of the same coin.

In this quotation, the writer reveals to his readers his principal argument ("my thesis"), the elements of the argument, and the way he will organize his discussion of the topic under consideration.

Writer-responsible writers also use prerevealing features at pivotal points throughout their texts. Tadros (1989), in her study of law and economics textbooks, provides a convenient taxonomy for identifying ways in which authors prereveal their content and organization, not only in the initial paragraphs of a text, but as the discourse changes or as the author feels that he or she needs to step outside the text and explain something to the reader. Her categories for these prerevealing elements are the following:

1. Enumeration ("There are two advantages to be derived from this method.")
2. Advance labeling ("Before discussing the questions further, however, it is necessary to define. . . .")
3. Reporting what others have said to introduce a topic ("A large part of economics is now devoted to a study of the problems of exchange, and Davenport emphasized this aspect when he declared. . . .")
4. Recapitulation of what has been said to introduce a new topic ("All the influences on location of industry so far considered have been economic in character.")
5. Hypotheticality ("Suppose that Dombey received a cheque from Nickleby, and both. . . .")
6. Rhetorical questions ("Why should we be interested in this topic?") (Adapted from Tadros, 1989, pp. 19–20)

Prerevealing is one aspect of *metadiscourse,* defined as the language in a text used when "the speaker/writer is situated above or outside of her own discourse, and is in a position to control and manipulate it" (Fairclough, 1992, p. 122). As Tadros found, some metadiscoursal features identify rhetorical actions or the functions of sections of the text with words such as *explain, demonstrate, claim.* Some features show divisions in the discourse, such as *first, second, third,* and some connect discourse parts with additives (*in addition, furthermore*), adversatives (*however, nevertheless*), or other conjuncts (see Halliday & Hasan, 1976; Williams, 1989, p. 28). The choice of metadiscoursal elements can be genre-sensitive, as I found when studying a collection of American English business letters (Johns, 1981a). In my data, the principal additive employed was *and,* and the only adversative was *but,* because the letters were written to general audiences with fairly low reading levels and limited reading time.

Thus, selection of readings texts can be made in terms of text-internal as well as text-external factors. By considering variety and student need in our selection, we can promote heightened genre awareness among our students.

Design carefully crafted writing assignments

Too many literacy classes are devoted to one kind of writing text, generally the pedagogical essay, written to a model in Traditional classrooms or by the principles of the Process Approach in others.[2] Students are not provided with assignment variety either in terms of prompt or genre. In addition, student texts are graded only by the literacy faculty rather than by others who might have different grading criteria. Literacy classrooms with one type of writing ("the essay") and one group of graders (literacy teachers) may be the only direct pedagogical experience that students have with producing English texts, even in English-speaking countries. Some literacy practitioners explain this lack of variety in their classes by arguing that "if you can write [or read] an essay, you can write [or read] anything." This is not generally the case, however. In these monogeneric classrooms, students become so familiar with pedagogical essays that they begin to believe that this is the only way to write, and this belief can present problems in both their academic and professional lives.

REQUIRING DIFFERENT GENRES, WRITER ROLES, AUDIENCES, AND PURPOSES

What are some of the possibilities for breaking out of a rigid literacy class mode? There are several. Students can write texts from different genres: summaries and abstracts, memos, editorials, love notes, recipes, and advertisements, to name a few. They can write for different, or more than one, purpose: to request, to complain, to compliment, to argue, or to critique. They can take on different roles as readers and writers. For example, they can act as critics and write to the authors of their textbooks about the problems or pleasures of the assigned readings. They can take on roles as graders and evaluators or the roles (and personalities) of other

2 See Chapter 1 for a discussion of Traditional and Psycholinguistic-Cognitive (Process) Approaches.

students in their literacy classes. They can also practice writing to different audiences. An assignment that is popular on our campus is to ask students to write two papers: one explaining a topic to a young member of the family and the other explaining the same topic to an unfamiliar faculty member. One of my colleagues assigns a letter to the editor of the campus newspaper and awards a high grade to any student whose letter is published. In other classes, students write to politicians, campus administrators, or to students outside of their classrooms. The Internet has opened a new door for addressing audiences: Students in different countries now write to each other by e-mail and learn a great deal about audience awareness, and language, as they do so.

IN DIFFERENT CONTEXTS AND UNDER VARYING CONSTRAINTS

Students can also be encouraged to write in and for different contexts, defined broadly as "the events that are going on around when people speak [and write]" (Bakhtin, 1986, p. 65). They can be asked to write down observations as they sit in the school cafeteria; they can be asked to write (and discuss) class notes in a lecture; they can be required to assess a literacy context in one of their classes and reflect upon that experience. Perhaps most important for student flexibility is the opportunity to read or write under various time constraints. For some assignments, students should go through the writing process: first draft, peer review, second draft, editing, etc.; in others, students should be asked to read or write quickly, under pressure.[3]

When considering context and constraints, we should also consider the type of assignment that is made. Students should have the opportunity to experience open-ended assignments ("Write about your previous semester") or assignments of their own choosing, but they should also experience a number of assignments that are very tightly written. Horowitz (1986a) and others have found that, outside literacy classes, writing prompts are often quite specific in detail, outlining the required organization, content, audience, conceptual framework, and detail (see Chapter 6).

INCLUDING A VARIETY OF CONVENTIONS AND VALUES

The concept of "genre" also encompasses form and conventions. Therefore, students need opportunities to read and write texts with a variety of formal features. Those expected to conduct research can study the

---

3 A faculty member on campus came to me one time and said, "Have students *never* written an in-class examination essay?" Because his students had come directly from high school experiences in which the "writing process" is central to literacy classes, they had had no experience with the kind of in-class timed essay response that is popular in many DS classes. As a result, they performed very poorly.

"moves" in article introductions (see Swales, 1990) and then attempt to replicate these moves when writing their texts. Students can read and study results sections of research papers and then attempt to write their own papers of this type. Other discourse forms, and their social importance, can be studied and written as appropriate: different types of letters from a variety of cultures, several types of timed essay examination responses, lab reports and lab notes, forms of poetry and stories. Students can also focus their study on the relationships between grammar and rhetorical function. They can study the use of the passive, the various forms of the present, the use of cohesion in particular types of texts, or syntactic choices (such as clefting or pseudo-clefting), and then attempt to use these forms in texts in a genre. In all cases, however, issues of form should be considered in terms of their functions within texts, the roles and purposes of the writer, and the rhetorical context.

Content can also be varied in literacy classes. Students can study the ways in which different authors deal with the same content, stressing some points and ignoring others in their argumentation. Then they can attempt to produce texts of their own that are partial in terms of content. Content can be discussed conceptually, as students create a conceptual tree for a group of readings within a subject area. Using this concept tree, they can summarize the important ideas related to a reading or discipline. Of course, content can also be studied in terms of vocabulary. Students can relate specific vocabulary words to the concept tree they have created for a class or to a single reading. They can scan for all the related vocabulary words in a text and discuss the relationships among these words in a written reflection. Another useful vocabulary exercise involves selection by student groups of the three most important vocabulary words in a reading, and then a defense of their choices in writing.[4] It is vital for students to deal with content issues in a variety of ways within a variety of texts and contexts, for content (and vocabulary) may be treated differently depending on the discipline, the classroom, the faculty member, and the assignment.

Students should also discuss and write about texts in terms of the values they represent. If a text is considered good writing by a faculty member or a professional, for example, the students can reflect on what makes it good: the argumentation, the use of disciplinary concepts, the organization, the register, the hedging, or other characteristics. Fully as important is student critique. My students speak of some of their assigned readings as "gobbledegook" because, in their view, the texts obfuscate argumentation, content, and organization, leaving them, as

---

4 They are not permitted to select words exclusively from the title. In some cases, the title may be omitted from the reading for this exercise.

readers, in the dust. In an article on the readability of academic writing, MacDonald (1990) makes the argument that scholars often employ sentence structure and terminology to obscure rather than to clarify. Using Joseph Williams's "grammar of clarity" (1989) as a measure, she demonstrates how a famous literary critic defies clarity standards with impunity. She then argues that professionals need to "think in terms of the social and cognitive consequences of readable versus less readable prose at varying levels of the academy" (p. 56). Like MacDonald, students need to think and write about why a text is unreadable for them. Is the vocabulary too difficult? Has the writer failed to follow Williams's rules for clarity? Is the syntax confusing? Is the text information-dense? If students can answer some of these questions, they can use their answers to critique academic texts.

If, as Briggs and Baumann (1992, p. 147) contend, "genre is quintessentially intertextual," then we need to give students a variety of intertextual writing experiences as well. Students can "reproduce" genre conventions from past discourses (see Berkenkotter & Huckin, 1995, p. 17). They can draw from library sources or elsewhere to give their texts authority through citation. They can draw from films or laboratory notes and interweave this information into their writing. In one of my classes in which "the research paper" is the topic, I assign five types of papers in which intertextuality plays a central role: a history assignment using resources from the library; a discourse analysis of a professional scientific article, in which citation is central; an examination and critique of visual texts such as propaganda posters or advertisements; a discussion and analysis of a family or cultural myth based on interviews; and a study of a rhetorical context using participant observation. As students complete each of these assignments, there is considerable classroom discussion of how readings, observations, interviews, or experiences can be woven into texts, and how this necessity for intertextuality affects student writing processes, their purposes, and their argumentation.

So far I have presented some basic tenets of a socioliterate curriculum, emphasizing the need to go into the world to conduct research and to invite others to our classrooms to broaden student understandings and sharpen their abilities to analyze and critique. Figure 1 provides a visual outline of these tenets.

In this chapter I have maintained that we need to select our reading texts and writing assignments with care, providing students with variety and challenge in terms of both text-external and text-internal features and opportunities to discuss and write about these characteristics in the classroom. Practitioners constrained by their teaching environment can still use some of the suggestions made here: Textbooks are socially constructed, for example, as are examination essays, and both can be analyzed and used for the advancement of genre knowledge.

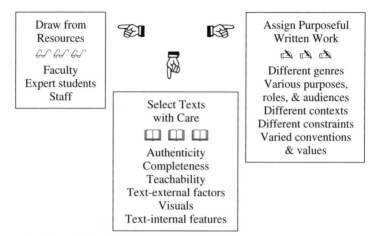

Figure 1   A socioliterate curriculum: Basic tenets.

Goals for students

What should our goals for a socioliterate classroom be? What particular skills and abilities, interests and motivations do we want our students to have when they leave our classrooms? This section is designed to suggest answers to these questions. The goals for students are listed and are followed by short commentaries. Students should be able to:

- *Draw from knowledge of genres and apply the knowledge to analysis and critique of known and new texts.* Our students come to the classroom with a great deal to offer in the study of the social construction of texts. Most have extensive genre knowledge about spoken and written texts when they arrive. They can name a variety of familiar texts and, if encouraged, they can discuss and critique many of the elements that are relevant to familiar genres. Chapters 2 and 3 listed the elements of genre knowledge and proposed the use of "homely" texts, such as wedding invitations and obituaries, to begin a classroom discussion. This discussion can assist students in developing ways to perform their own genre analyses on texts from less familiar contexts. Thus students need to practice applying their own knowledge of genres in our classes and need to be encouraged to consider this knowledge, and its implications, when confronting academic textual experiences.
- *Perpetually revise theories of genre.* An issue raised frequently in the literature is that every text encountered will be different from previous texts, even from those in the same genre. In the "homely" genre catego-

ries, such as recipes or obituaries, in the pedagogical categories, such as school essays or term papers, in the academic professional categories, such as grants and research articles, changes from one text to another are almost certain to take place as the texts are revised for specific situations. Predictably, content will change, but other genre features, such as form and reader and writer roles, may change as well. Thus it is very important that students not have fixed genre theories, but instead, that their theories be constantly open to revision. We need to assist students in assessing rhetorical contexts and the texts within them for those elements that are similar to, or different from, previously encountered analogous situations, therefore enabling them constantly to revise their theories of genre.

- *Assess, expand upon, and revise strategies for approaching literacy tasks.* Our students bring with them particular strategies for approaching the reading and writing of texts, based on their own theories of literacy. Some students read every text slowly, word for word; they may write in the same way, carefully selecting each word before going on. Other students "undermonitor" all of their work, reading quickly without comprehending well or writing swiftly and neglecting to edit. Students need to assess their current strategies in terms of their success in completing different types of literacy tasks. In some cases, word-for-word reading may be the best approach; in others, very quick text skimming may be more useful. There is no one "writing process" or "reading process" but many, and students need to be open to a myriad of possibilities as they advance in their academic and professional careers.

  After assessing their current approaches to literacy, students should develop additional ones, by interviewing other students about their strategies, by trying out different possibilities, or by reading about strategies undertaken by successful students. After having explored their already-established approaches and learned about more, they can attempt various types of reading and writing to see which strategies work with different tasks.

  Students must leave our classes with strategy repertoires that are more extensive than those with which they entered. They also need to be aware that different strategies work for different tasks: No one approach will be successful in all situations. We must give them practice in strategy revision, expansion, and evaluation, so that they can be better prepared to meet a variety of literacy challenges.

- *Develop abilities to research and critique texts, roles, and contexts.* Our students must be researchers and critics, into their past genre knowledge and strategies and into specific contexts in which texts are central. We need to encourage and honor careful student research and critique, and urge students to continue in these efforts throughout their adult lives. Like all researchers, students need to pose questions (In reading: "Who wrote this text? For whom? What do – or don't – I understand about the text? How do the text features fulfill the writer's or the community's needs? What values are embedded? Do I agree with them? How are the content and argumentation presented? Why? What are the weaknesses or deficiencies in the text?" In writing: "What are the elements of the task that has been assigned? Can I negotiate them? How? How can I break these elements down to make a plan for writing? Who is my audience? What are my purposes? What steps shall I take in completing this text?") As researchers, students need to test their hypotheses against previous genre and task experiences and against the advice of others. Good readers and writers, particularly of difficult texts, are always involved in literacy research.

Through research, intelligent critique can be encouraged. It is not sufficient for students to say that a reading text is "gobbledegook," for example. They need to be able to identify those features of the text that make it difficult for them to read. By the same token, they cannot criticize a writing assignment until they have researched its weaknesses. Critique is valuable and empowering; well designed and presented to a faculty or professional audience, it can convince even the most skeptical.

- *Cultivate a metalanguage about texts and textual experiences.* Having a metalanguage, or a language about language, permits students to distance themselves from experiences or texts and discuss them with considerable objectivity. Many students, particularly in EFL contexts, have already developed a sophisticated metalanguage about grammar. They can name the parts of speech, talk about tense and aspect, and discuss various syntactic possibilities. This grammatical metalanguage is very useful as they analyze forms and their functions in genres. However, students need to develop additional metalanguages as well: about the moves and macrostructures of texts, about semantic categories of vocabulary words, about content and concepts, and about other text-internal and text-external features of genres. It is also useful for students to develop a language about their strategies for completing tasks, thus enabling them to discuss, critique, and reflect upon what they have done and how they have done it and to assess their successes and failures.

☑ To draw from knowledge of genres and apply this knowledge to analysis and critique of known and new texts.

☑ To perpetually revise theories of genre.

☑ To assess, expand upon, and revise strategies for approaching literacy tasks.

☑ To develop abilities to research and critique texts, roles, and contexts.

☑ To cultivate a metalanguage about texts and textual experiences.

☑ To reflect on experiences with texts, roles, and contexts.

Figure 2   Literacy goals for students.

- *Reflect on experiences with texts, roles, and contexts.* As readers will discover, reflection, in both discussion and writing, is central to approaches described in this volume. Reflection assists students to summarize and understand what they have done, assess their work, and make plans for change. It assists them to examine texts in new and critical ways, and to revise their theories about genres. Not incidentally, classroom reflection assists teachers, because they can revise their curricula as they identify student needs and wants. My students reflect constantly, and they find it to be one of the most positive and lasting experiences in their literacy classes.

Figure 2 summarizes the goals for students in a socioliterate curriculum, many of which have been discussed at greater length in earlier chapters.

In this chapter, I have set the stage for the remainder of the volume, which is devoted to pedagogical applications. I have outlined some general tenets of a socioliterate approach and then listed some goals for students, particular abilities or interests they should be encouraged to carry from our classrooms into other contexts, so that their literacies may continue to evolve and mature. I have suggested that not all these tenets or goals can be put into practice in all environments; however, in any context, teachers and students can develop analytical attitudes that can motivate research and reflection.

In her study of strategies used by ESL writers in academic classes, Leki (1995, p. 255) notes that "it is potentially worrisome that the . . . students enrolled in ESL classes at the beginning of the term never referred to links between what they did there and what they were required to do in other classes." This *is* worrisome, for if we are to teach academic literacies, we should make concerted efforts to link what we do to the communities of practice in our universities. We need to heighten student awareness of the complexity of text production and enable them to analyze, critique, plan, and reflect in ways that ensure continuing evolution of their literacies and of their theories of genres throughout their lives.

8 Putting tenets and goals into practice
Using portfolios in literacy classrooms

A portfolio is a collection of my specific written works: four different assignments. By using this system, I can see my improvement in writing, and it makes me feel more responsible for doing the several tasks. It also helps me to think about different kinds of papers (Nguyen Hoa, student, developmental writing class at San Diego State University, December 1991).

In many ESL writing classes, teachers purposely structure writing assignments for success. . . . [However], if writing successes come too easily, they may be insufficiently challenging to serve the purpose of giving students writing experiences they can later refer back to in attempting to address tasks across the curriculum. Although ESL [or any literacy] class should no doubt be psychologically nurturing place, surely being a safe refuge is not enough (Leki, 1995, p. 256).

Throughout this volume, it has been argued that students should have a variety of motivating and challenging text experiences in their literacy classes, and that they should view texts and, to some extent, their strategies and processes for achieving tasks, as socially constructed. This chapter discusses classroom approaches that attempt to apply this argument, using the principles and goals outlined in the previous chapter.

Portfolios are becoming of increasing interest to literacy practitioners. These tools are flexible in terms of content, size, and purpose, so they may be adapted to many teaching and learning contexts. In addition, they are uniquely suited to expose students to a variety of genres. Portfolios also encourage students to reflect upon their own tasks and textual experiences, their processes, and their strategies (see especially Belanoff & Dickson, 1991; Black et al., 1994; Frazier & Paulson, 1992; Purves et al., 1995; Tierney et al., 1991). Because of the many possibilities for portfolios within a broad spectrum of literacy classrooms, this chapter is devoted to the following questions:

1. What are the basic features of literacy portfolios?
2. How can portfolios be managed?
3. What are some of the possibilities for different types of portfolio designs? For classes in which reading is the goal, for example? For writing classes? For mixed-skills classes?

4. In what specific ways can literacy and discipline-specific classes be linked through portfolios?

Literacy portfolios: Basic features

What are the necessary components of literacy portfolios? Although there are many possible variations, certain basic features apply in almost every case:

1. *Most portfolios are in notebook form, assembled, over time, by the students.* Portfolio notebooks (or folders) are divided into carefully marked off core entry sections, each of which contains the core entry itself (a student paper, a genre exemplar, a special reading, a picture) and additional materials related to the entry. These materials might include the various plans and drafts of an entry paper ("the whole process"), comments by other students or the instructor on the core entry, or a student reflection.

2. *They are collections of literacy artifacts.* What is collected will depend, of course, on program goals. Many types of collections are discussed in the portfolio literature: of readings; of writings; of visual items such as pictures, graphs, or charts; or of work in students' first and second languages. Often, portfolio entries provide a mix of these artifacts.

3. *Core entries are selected; usually there are no more than five for a school term.* Rather than include everything read or written during a term, portfolios contain representative samples. In most programs, curriculum designers determine the core entry categories in advance, thereby providing a structure for the literacy program. In some programs the students select the items that will be entered for each category. In others the instructors select the particular items that will be included. Sometimes, selection is shared among teachers and students.

A few literacy portfolios contain only one entry, perhaps a long research paper and all of the intertextual items related to it. It is more common for portfolios to contain several entries; however, requiring more than five selected entries during a school term can lead to classroom management difficulties.

4. *The entries and reflections represent the goals of the literacy program.* One of the major benefits of portfolios is that they can embody the core elements of any literacy program: its goals, its texts, its tasks, or its examinations. In many literacy classes, working with portfolios is a constant reminder to students and teachers of the goals of the program and how they are being accomplished through literacy experiences.

5. *Portfolios are assembled over time.* Some portfolios are designed for a single school term. Others are designed for more than one term or to

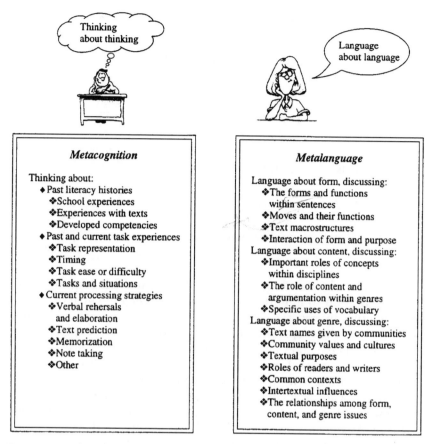

Figure 1   The "metas."

include entries from throughout a students' education in a particular institution.[1] Whatever the case, the over-time feature is an important one, because it permits students to observe changes in their texts and literacy practices and to reflect upon these changes for several months.[2]

6. *Portfolios require reflection.* One of the several differences between portfolios and other collections of student work is that the former require students to think and talk about their entries and write about how a

1 On our campus, we have a single, elaborate portfolio that future teachers compile containing material from each of their major classes and "connections essays," reflections that link the class material with their teaching.
2 When I conducted a portfolio workshop in Singapore, the participants reminded me that not all students *progress*. But they probably will change over time, and these changes should be matters for reflection.

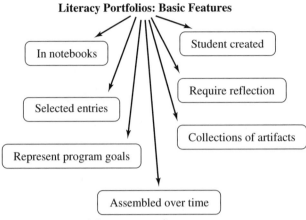

Figure 2   Literacy portfolios: Basic features.

particular entry is related to their literate lives or to other texts in a genre. Why is reflection so important? It is often designed to enhance student metacognitive awareness. Through reflections, students are encouraged to think about their representation of tasks, the social forces influencing their texts, and how they employed strategies to complete tasks. Because portfolios are compiled over time, students can also reflect upon their changes in attitude toward their own reading and writing, toward their audiences, toward academic English, or toward other factors that are important to their literate lives. Reflection also enhances students' meta-language. As students discuss texts and text features in their reflections, they become increasingly comfortable in using a "language about language" to discuss their work. Thus, reflection should be an essential feature of any portfolio design. Figure 1 reviews the areas of metacognition ("thinking about thinking") and metalanguage ("language about language") that can be important to student reflection.

Most instructors ask students to reflect in writing during class. They do not grade reflections or correct them for errors; thus reflections are more like journal entries than like finished, edited products.

7. *Portfolios can, and often do, integrate curriculum and assessment.* Essential to many portfolio programs are the evaluation procedures, which, many would argue, are fairer to students than more traditional approaches. Rather than being assessed by one examination, students can be evaluated continuously, as is the case in some programs; or their end-of-term evaluation can be based on their entire portfolio rather than on a single paper. No single test or paper determines a student's literacy or grades.

8. *Portfolios provide an organized, student-created record of learning and accomplishment.* Students at all levels can develop a pride of ownership in their portfolios. Some students decorate them quite elaborately, and many take them as souvenirs when they have finished their literacy classes. Portfolios can represent an important element in students' academic lives, an attractive document showing where they have been and where they may be going.

Figure 2 shows in a visual manner the basic features of portfolios.

Portfolio management

One of the many advantages of portfolio design is that it can encourage instructors to discuss program theories, pedagogies, and requirements with each other and with program administrators before the semester begins and during various examination periods. If these discussions do not take place, and instructors begin their portfolio classes without careful planning, all of those concerned may be disappointed. An issue that must be discussed among program planners in advance is management, the basic design and organization of portfolios in the classes. This is one fairly standard list of management issues, developed during the literacy program discussions on our campus:

1. Portfolios must be compiled in a three-ring folder with a tab representing each core entry.
2. There should be five entries for a 45-hour literacy class offered during a single university term.
3. Each entry must be introduced by a reflection, written in class. Reflections may be scripted with questions or open-ended.
4. The order of core entries must be identical for all members of the class, although entry due dates (which are affixed to the front of the folder) can vary from class to class.
5. A set of guidelines and core entry due dates written by the instructor must be included in the front cover of the folder.
6. Students may select representative samples for the core entries to include. Each of these entries will be evaluated before they are entered into the portfolio. With instructor permission, students can revise or replace these entries to improve their grades.
7. Students should be encouraged to take pride in their portfolios. They may decorate them or improve their visual appearance through the use of special computer fonts or clip art.
8. Portfolios should be completed by the end of the term. Only complete

portfolios, with all entries and reflections included, will be considered for final assessment.[3]

These guidelines provide one fairly successful attempt at management, but they are evaluated and revised each semester. The important point of this discussion is that teachers and students must have some management principles to go on as they work with their portfolios throughout the term.

Generic portfolio models

The possibilities for literacy portfolio designs are many. Each program, each instructor, and each class may have different goals, core entries, and directions for reflection. However, in socioliterate practice, two program goals are stable and consistent. The first is that every entry should be conspicuously different from every other in terms of the textual, contextual, and/or socioliterate forces that influence it. Second, entry titles should be generative, not constrictive. Portfolios should encourage invention and diversity within core entry types. Thus, the titles for core entries should be designed to be sufficiently open-ended to allow for considerable classroom flexibility.

Two basic portfolio models will be described here. These designs are intended for literacy classes that are free-standing, not linked to specific types of classes or classrooms. They are sufficiently open-ended to be adapted to a large variety of programs.

Model one: A reading portfolio

In some parts of the world, especially in EFL contexts, reading is sometimes the only literacy skill in a curriculum. A portfolio that focuses on reading alone is thus the only alternative. The entries suggested here can be used with academic students at all but the most basic English proficiency levels. If students have difficulty writing, reflection can be accomplished through class discussion. Because students bring with them considerable textual knowledge from their first languages and schooling experiences, they can recognize and talk about some genres with little difficulty, whatever their level. Of course, what is required, in both the core entry and the reflection, will vary depending on context, student academic and proficiency levels, the curriculum and examinations, and text availability. For students entering graduate programs, for example,

---

3 Portfolio principles: Department of Rhetoric and Writing Studies (RW 100), Fall 1994.

instructors might replace the textbook entries suggested here with texts from the academic genres of the students' chosen disciplines.

What entries might be included in a reading portfolio?

ENTRY 1: TWO PRIMARY COMMUNITY TEXTS FROM THE SAME GENRE

The first core entries can be from the students' primary cultures and languages. These entries will encourage their first efforts to integrate language, texts, contexts, and participant purposes in their genre analyses. Several first-culture "homely" discourses have been suggested elsewhere in this volume; however, there are many other possibilities that students can enter into their portfolios and reflect upon. If the students are completely at sea when assigned this entry, teachers can encourage them to bring newspapers or magazines from their homes, shops, or neighborhoods, or they can ask students to copy from posted handbills or graffiti and use these as their texts.

Reflection: Since many students are not accustomed to reflecting upon texts, the first reflections of the term can be scripted with a number of questions. Students can complete written (or spoken) answers to one or more of the following: "What are the texts you have chosen called? Who writes them? Why? Who reads them? Why? What are the features of these two named texts that may make them typical? How are the texts different from each other? Why?"

ENTRY 2: TWO TEXTBOOK ENTRIES

The next entries can be two readings from textbooks or assigned curricula.[4] These paired text entries can be duplicated copies from two textbooks on the same subject that describe the same phenomenon or concept. Or, if students have access to only one textbook, they can use as their entries two examples from the text aids, such as the questions at the back of the chapter, and discuss in their reflections how these questions are similar to each other, what kinds of answers they require ("facts," "synthesis"), and whether they are appropriate for a particular academic class. Students can also use materials from their literacy classes for comparison. For example, they can analyze the ways in which features of English grammar are explained in textbooks, or they can compare several definitions of related terms from a glossary. Selecting any set of paired discourses encourages students to make comparisons about how texts are realized for specific purposes in particular contexts.

Students can also include two charts, graphs, formulas, or other non-linear features from the same or different textbooks, comparing them in

---

4 Students who are not yet enrolled in academic classes can collect these samples from faculty experts, other students, or the library.

their reflections and suggesting how they are designed to help the reader to understand a concept or process. Students can include parts of the textbook that explain the core concepts or processes of the discipline. Whatever the choices, the entries should also be designed to encourage better understanding of the topic or subject matter of a course, to engender discussions of social forces influencing the texts, or to stimulate a comparisons of lexis, grammar, or argumentation.

Reflection: As is the case in all reflections, the questions posed should reflect the literacy program's goals for students. Questions such as the following can be asked: "For whom are these textbooks written? How do you know? Who wrote them? Do they have authority in the discipline? In what ways do all textbooks appear to be alike? In what ways do they differ? What particular features of textbooks do you find useful? If you were writing a textbook to help others learn your chosen discipline (or English), how would you organize the chapters (or a discussion of a grammatical feature)?"

If a more text-internal analytical approach is preferred, students can respond to these questions: How are the questions formed in the textbook aids section? What is the syntax of these questions? How are the visuals alike or different from each other? Are they useful to you as a reader? Why or why not? How are the headings related to the core concepts of the course?

ENTRY 3: TWO SUMMARIES OR ABSTRACTS

Summarizing is one of the most common strategies required of academic readers. However, many students, and some instructors, do not recognize that there are various types of summaries in academic texts (Ratterey, 1985). To encourage this understanding, students can collect summaries of various types: the linear pedagogical summaries that follow the organization of a text, summaries that also critique, reformulated, and one-sentence summaries. They can also collect visual summaries: the illustrations used in texts to summarize information such as those in this volume. Two summaries of the same type can be included in the entry, or two different types may be chosen.

Reflection: Questions for reflections will, as usual, depend on program goals. Here are some possibilities: "How are the summaries organized? What topics are mentioned first? Second? Why do you think that these summaries are organized in this manner? What do you notice about the language of these texts? Is paraphrase used? What kinds of verbs predominate? [And] What strategies do you use to prepare a summary? What do you do first, second . . . ? How do you think the writers of these summaries planned as they wrote these texts?"[5]

5 These are also good questions for visiting faculty and expert students.

ENTRY 4: A READER'S CHOICE

Whereas the three previous core entry types are chosen by the instructor, this entry represents individual student choice. Here, one text for the entry is sufficient, because the principal purposes are to require students to reflect upon turning points in their literacy histories or important texts in their communities. I give these instructions for entry selection: "Select a text you have read that has been very important to you personally, to your family or community, or to your education. The selection can be in your first language or in English."

Students make interesting choices for this category; and their reflections, which are open-ended and unscripted, are generally very good. Here are some examples from my classes. From their first languages, students chose a poem, an obituary of a relative, advertisements for herbal remedies, and an official document from their home country. Some of the English entries included the first text read and understood in English, a test, a page from a drivers' manual, and a page from their favorite textbook.

Reflection: I find that students need very little direction in reflecting upon their reader's choice. I ask: "What is this text called? How can it be described? Why is this important to you, to your literacy education or practices, or to your language, culture, or community?"

ENTRY 5: A DIFFICULT (OR EASY) READING

This entry also consists of one rather than two texts and focuses on students' current literacy abilities. Instructions are the following: "Choose one English language reading that is (or has been) particularly difficult (or easy) for you to read. Make a copy (or copy a page) for your entry."

Reflection: Possible questions are: What is this reading called? Where is it taken from? Who wrote it? What do we know about the purposes, community, first language, and values of the writer? For whom is it written? For what reasons do you find this reading particularly difficult (or easy)? Be specific. Answers to these reflection questions assist students to consider their progress in reading, their reading strategies, and the features of the particular reading tasks that they have found to be difficult (or easy).

This five-entry portfolio model is one of many possibilities in a literacy situation in which reading is central. It represents an effort to elicit from students their text histories, their current understandings of the situated nature of texts, their awareness of the social forces that influence texts, and their understanding that the strategies for text processing will vary according to many factors within a rhetorical situation. Modified, this model can be used in many environments for students at a variety of academic or proficiency levels.

Model two: A writing portfolio

For this second design, I am indebted to participants from a Portfolio Workshop I conducted for the Singapore Tertiary English Teachers' Society (November 1993). One group of participants[6] designed a writing portfolio for the General Paper (GP) A Level Students, EFL students who were advanced in terms of both proficiency and academic level and who were constrained by curricular and examination conditions. Despite the constraints, the reflection questions are excellent, demonstrating the creativity that can exist even within a set curriculum. Here are the entries and reflection questions.

ENTRY 1: A TIMED PIECE (ARGUMENTATIVE, EXPOSITORY, OR REFLECTIVE)

During the class, instructors asked students to write several timed essays, because their final examination would also be timed. Among the timed essays administered, each student was asked to include one as the core entry.

Reflection: Designers created reflection questions for each entry type. For those students who selected the argumentative essay, for example, the following guided their responses: "Write in your own words your interpretation of the question. How did you remain relevant to this question as you wrote? How did you balance both sides of the argument depending on the focus of the questions? How effective do you think it was in helping you to answer the question? How did you decide upon dividing your paragraphs? What was your main problem in writing this essay and how did you solve it? To what extent did you make use of other resources in your writing? What words or phrases did you particularly like? Are you satisfied with what you wrote? Why or why not?" As can be seen, these questions were carefully scripted to meet the needs of the students and course goals. From student answers, instructors could focus on particular areas of difficulty as the students prepared for their final timed examinations central to their future academic placement.

ENTRY 2: A RESEARCH-BASED PROJECT USING A PROCESS APPROACH

For this entry, literacy students were assigned a short library research paper by the instructor. They had to include the final paper and all of their materials leading to the final product ("the whole process").

---

6 In this group were Jayanti Veronique Banerjee, Lydia Tanchia, Rick Ussher, Chan Chee Har, Shie Jie, and Robert Foo, all instructors or supervisors from Singapore community colleges.

Reflection: Students were asked to respond to some of the following questions: "What timing and other goals did you set for this paper? What particular difficulties did you encounter when attempting to complete the paper? How could these difficulties be overcome when you write your next paper? What successes did you have? What did you learn from your successes? How do you like your final product? Why?" In this case, instructors were particularly interested in issues such as task representation and in how the strategies undertaken influenced the students' successes and failures.

ENTRY 3: A SUMMARY

Throughout the semester in this literacy program, the students were required to prepare summaries of readings. Among them, they were to choose one for an entry.

Reflection: Questions included the following: "Why did you select this summary among the several that you have written? How is it organized? Why is it organized in this manner? If you were asked by another person to define a summary, what would you say? What are the basic elements of all of the summaries you have written?"

ENTRY 4: A WRITER'S CHOICE

Students were given this "wild card" as an open-ended possibility for their portfolios. They were to choose something they had written in their first language or English that had been important to their personal or school literacy lives.

Reflection: The following questions guided the reflections: "What is this? When and where did you write it? For whom? Why did you make this choice? What does it tell us about you as a literate person?"

ENTRY 5: AN OVERALL REFLECTION ON THE PORTFOLIO PROGRAM

In many portfolio designs there is a general reflection that integrates all of the entries and discusses program goals. This general type was required as the last, culminating entry for the portfolio. In completing this reflection, students were asked: "What were the goals of this class? Describe each entry in the portfolio and discuss why it is important to these goals."

This writing portfolio has a particular design to meet the needs of a group of A-level students in an EFL context. However, as in the case of the reading portfolio, the core entry categories and reflection questions are sufficiently generative to be suitable for many other pedagogical situations as well.

Model three: A mixed-skills portfolio from a linked class

I now turn to my own situation, one in which a portfolio provides the structure for a linked-class[7] content-based instruction program. Though I describe a particularly ideal situation within a supportive context, I hope that what is discussed here will provide both hope and inspiration for those who design linked classes or develop portfolios that enhance socioliterate practices. Throughout this volume I have argued that we must continuously work toward mediation and cooperation, toward placing our students in specific classroom situations and helping them to analyze the social forces around them. The results of one effort toward these goals are described here.

Since 1985, my colleagues and I at San Diego State University (California), a large, comprehensive public institution, have been attempting to bring the pedagogical principles described in this volume into practice. The curriculum for which we are responsible is now part of the larger, campus-wide Freshman Success Program (FSP), designed for first-year university students, many of whom are ESL, bilingual, and/or bicultural. In the linked class portion of the FSP, called the Integrated Curriculum (IC), students are divided into cohorts of twenty to twenty-five, based on their English language test scores. Each cohort is enrolled in a literacy ("writing") class appropriate to their level,[8] a discipline-specific class such as introductory biology, sociology, anthropology, political science, or history, a study group led by a graduate student from the discipline, and a University Seminar class, an orientation course taught by university faculty and administrators (see Figure 2 in Chapter 5). Both the Integrated Curriculum and the University Seminar are related administratively to the Department of Rhetoric and Writing Studies.

When we first designed the linked class program for developmental students in 1985,[9] we began to talk about the portfolio syllabus for the literacy class that would be most appropriate to our 15-week (45-hour)

---

7 Readers may remember that the term "adjunct" may be used in other environments for the linked class concept.

8 These are called writing classes, because writing is the only literacy skill required and tested by the university. A few less proficient students also enroll in a reading class. Whether students enroll for writing only or for writing and reading, all four skills (listening, speaking, reading, and writing) are included in the program. Our research (Johns, 1981b) has shown that reading and listening are actually more important to undergraduate academic success than writing or speaking.

9 "Developmental" is the word we use for any students who have not passed the first-year writing competency examination and are therefore considered to be writing below the freshman proficiency level. In other contexts, these students are called "remedial." Many of the students speak English as a second language.

term. Following our tradition of mediating between our department and the campus, we turned to the college deans[10] and asked that they poll their faculty about the "kinds of reading and writing" most common in undergraduate classes. We were interested in naming, which is important to understanding of genres and discourse communities (Swales, 1990), and in what kinds of texts were associated with these names. As indicated in Chapter 2, however, naming of pedagogical genres is problematic. Faculty responded that they required "a research (or term) paper," or "essay examinations," or that students were required to read from textbooks. This did not tell us very much, because we had very little to go on in terms of the features of these genres.[11] Thus, we took an approach in which our portfolio entries identified strategies for developing texts across genres. We hoped that by moving in this direction, we would both reflect the interests of our colleagues across campus and provide for literacy instructors, some of whom are graduate students or novice, temporary faculty, both guidance and flexibility. Keeping the goals listed in Chapter 7 in mind, we devised a developmental ESL (DE) syllabus outline consisting of five core portfolio entries: a summary or abstract, a data-driven paper, a source-driven paper, a timed, in-class essay response, and a wild card.

Here I will discuss one experience with this portfolio, in which my literacy class was linked with a history course taught by a faculty member whose concern for student learning is evident in her extensive syllabus and her stated interest in "including the students in the disciplinary conversation."[12] Because of her continuing concern for student learning, we agreed to co-construct our syllabi, deciding that, during the term, her papers and oral presentations would overlap with mine. She appeared as a history expert in my class; I made guest appearances in her class as a literacy expert, suggesting how to read the various sources required (novels, original sources, a textbook), how to take notes, how the students might break into manageable parts the difficult tasks the professor assigned.

This section describes some of our cooperative efforts, including the literacy and history assignments that were co-constructed for the syllabus. Though I will not write in detail about each of the portfolio entries in my literacy class, the readers can infer from the co-construction efforts the importance of this linked class effort: to the students, to the faculty

---

10 Our university is organized by colleges, each of which includes a number of academic departments. These are Arts and Letters, Business Administration, Education, Engineering, Health and Human Services, Professional Studies and Fine Arts, and Sciences.

11 See Chapter 2 for a discussion of the problems posed by pedagogical genres.

12 Her name is Elizabeth Colwill, a *wonderful* professor!

involved, and, not incidentally, to other faculty with whom we continue to discuss this cooperative venture.

Before this "linking" semester began, the history professor and I discussed how we might integrate our classes in a manner that was transparent to the students. In preparation, we shared our goals. I listed the goals outlined in Chapter 6 of this volume. She told me that her goals for students are:

1. Interpretation, backed by argumentation with the uses of sources as data. ("History *is* interpretation.")
2. Effective note taking: building on the outline and vocabulary presented in class.
3. Integration of information from notes with information and argumentation in the readings [intertextuality].
4. Reading for different purposes, in this case, for the questions and problems central to the history class.[13]
5. Speaking and listening: formulating questions, volunteering answers, making presentations, effective role-playing.

In the list provided by this instructor, we find many of the important elements of academic literacy: the management of sources (1–3), reading and interpreting different genres for different purposes (4), and exploiting spoken and written texts to achieve a variety of academic tasks (3 and 5).

From the two lists, we developed our syllabi, each of which required a portfolio. The history instructor's portfolio included responses and reflections, selected from weekly reading assignments. I required a portfolio that followed the syllabus for all literacy classes at this level. In the following section, I will indicate through assignments and literacy portfolio entries some of the ways in which the two classes were integrated.

ENTRY 1: A SOURCE-DRIVEN PAPER

The history assignment was as follows:

LIBRARY RESEARCH (20% of final history class grade). "How does the world of Juan Cabezon of Castille in the novel *1492* differ from the culture in which you were raised?"

The final product (due on xxx), should consist of four parts:

1) Describe your research process and list the research tools (books, computers, academic journals . . . no encyclopedias, please) that you used to locate historical sources that help you to respond to this question.

---

13 Her texts included three novels, *1492* (a picturesque novel by Homer Aridijis), *Frankenstein* (by Mary Shelley), and *Wretched of the Earth* (by Franz Fanon).

2) List six sources (three from books and three from journals) that you located and read. Star the ones that were most useful.

3) Develop a thesis (also called an argument or position statement) in response to the question listed above that draws from *1492* and your library sources.

4) In one page, write or diagram a PLAN for your research paper. In this plan, use your sources (quoted or paraphrased with author and page number listed in parentheses) to support your argument. (Use *Chicago Manual* style for citation and referencing.)

In the literacy class, the portfolio entry included a copy of this process-based history assignment and a completed paper on this topic, with the drafts, and peer reviews and my instructor comments. In my class, then, the students prepared the term paper of three to five pages from what they had begun in history, producing two drafts, submitting them to peer and instructor review, developing criteria for scoring, and submitting a final edited paper for a literacy grade. The best papers written for my class were selected by student groups and shared with the history professor.

In the literacy portfolio reflection, the students were asked to answer one or more of the following questions in two pages.

1) What did you already know about writing research papers (using sources) when you entered your history and composition classes? Had you thought about how to organize a paper like this? How did you find out how to organize it?

2) What did you learn from completing Dr. Colwill's assignment? How did you represent the task before you began it? What kinds of successes and difficulties did you have in using the library? Was making a plan a good idea? How did you go about writing the plan she required?

3) How did you go about writing a paper developed from the plan? Did you have to replan? Of what benefit were the drafts and peer reviews?

4) Examine your first, second and third drafts of the paper. What changes did you make in each draft? Were they changes in organization? In content? In grammar or punctuation? Be specific.

5) Was your paper written in academic language appropriate to your history class? Why or why not? Did it help the reader to read through use of cohesion and other elements?

6) What about the paper shows that it is uniquely yours? How were you able to use the assignment to achieve your own ends?

7) What is good about the final draft of your paper? What could you still improve if time permitted?

ENTRY 2: A SUMMARY OR ABSTRACT

The history assignment was as follows:

GROUP WORK CULMINATING IN PRESENTATION (30%)
These were the instructions from the syllabus: A significant body of research has shown that cooperative learning produces higher rates of

academic achievement than do traditional forms of instruction[14] (In my experience, it's also more fun.) In this class, you will each have the opportunity to participate in a work group that will meet for various purposes throughout the semester. Your work group will also get together outside of class time to research and prepare a presentation for the entire class. The goal is to teach one another and to enjoy the process.

After I assign you to a group, you will select a topic for your presentation from the options listed in the syllabus. In your half-hour presentation, your group must explore the topic that I have suggested, but you have a great deal of leeway on the format. Use your imagination in designing your performance. For instance, make a video, play music, present your art, show slides, plan a debate in which the whole class participates, stage a play with historical characters. The day of your presentation, your group will turn in a collective, two-page typed reflection on your preparation for the performance. How did members of your group work together? How often did you meet? Who attended the meetings? What roles did each person assume in the group and research process?

Keep these objectives in mind:

Get an early start on your research!
Use regular meeting times for your group.
Work collaboratively.
Think historically.
Present your ideas imaginatively (NO book reports please. Your goal is to educate classmates, not put them to sleep!)
Involve each member of the group (and perhaps even the class) in your presentation.

Grades: You can earn up to 15 points for active, cooperative, and consistent participation in your group over the course of the semester. (Your group's two-page assessment will play a role in determining the number of points that you receive.) The performance itself, for which you will be graded as a group, is worth 15 points.

The literacy class assignment led students to examine a genre with which many were already familiar, the critical summary and review. I asked students to collect copies of movie and book reviews from publications they had seen or read.[15] We hypothesized about "old" or expected generic elements of these reviews, comparing several. Then we talked about how these texts were different, depending on the writers' purposes, the community, and the other rhetorical factors that influence situated texts. We discussed organization, language, metamessages, and other factors that aid readers in processing texts.

After these discussions, I gave the students this prompt:

Write a summary and critique of your presentation in the Western Civilization class. Your audience is your history professor. In one type-written page,

14 I had provided the instructor with a number of articles on cooperative learning, on which she based much of her planning.
15 They were permitted to collect reviews in their first languages, but they had to bring their own translations.

discuss the purposes of the presentation, summarize what you did, and critique your presentation, basing your arguments upon the goals of the history class. (See Dr. C's assignment.)

The students completed the reflections and then turned in their summary/critiques to both the history instructor and to me.

In their reflections upon this summary/critique, students were to answer this question:

We often summarize. Discuss one summary you have given to others (either orally or in writing) in the recent past. How was this summary/critique alike – or different from – the summary you just completed about your presentation? Why?

ENTRY 3: A GENRE FROM THE DISCIPLINE

For the history assignment, students were assigned to read and reflect in their reading responses upon a number of first-person accounts of historical events taken from their collection of original sources. The reflections on these readings were part of the history portfolio.

To prepare for the literacy assignment, students returned to the volume of original sources assigned in the history class to identify the readings that were first-person accounts. The students worked in groups to examine several, talking about what the accounts had in common (in addition to using the first person) and how they differed. As a class, we talked about the use of the narratives in these accounts, about organization, about grammar and style, about writer orientation, audience, and argumentation. Because this paper was assigned late in the term, students were much more astute about genre analysis than they had been earlier; I was impressed by the sophistication of their discussions. When we were finished analyzing the texts taken from the history class, the students wrote their own first-person accounts, using this prompt:

Each person is an actor in history, whether it be in a local event or a more important event, reported in the newspapers. Prepare a first-person account in which you show how *you* were an actor in history. First, give us the background for the event. Then tell us, in narrative form, the story of your involvement. Then analyze your experience as you look back upon it.

When I first gave the assignment, students began to worry about whether they had been actors in history, so we explored possibilities. Once we had included attending large rock concerts, protesting anti-immigration measures on the state ballot, participating in a large meeting reported in the paper, and witnessing (or taking part in) a crime, the students realized that they had, in fact, been involved in making history. Their accounts were, for the most part, very good; this became one of their favorite assignments. The student groups selected papers to share with the history professor, who enjoyed reading them.

ENTRY 4: A READING FROM THE DISCIPLINE-SPECIFIC CLASS

For the fourth entry, students were not given the usual latitude. Because both the history professor and I realized that the variety of genres required in her history class (textbook, novels, and original sources) presented difficulties for the students, I decided that this category should include a copy of the first page of one of the history readings required during the semester.

Reflection: In their reflection upon the reading chosen, the students answered the following question:

Why did you select this single reading for your portfolio? Was it difficult for you? Why? Was it the most interesting? Why? Reread the entire reading and discuss particular passages that you find most important to your development as a reader or historian.

What did you learn about or from this reading that you did not know before?

ENTRY 5: A TIMED ESSAY

Students took a timed essay in the literacy class to practice a strategy that is very common in their DS classes: reading a prompt with specific directions and responding to it within a given time period. The prompt was based upon those from their history class.

The reflection question was the following:

How was this timed essay experience somewhat the same as or different from the other writing you've been doing in your composition and history classes? In your answer, pay particular attention to the language and organization of your text and your writing processes.

What is the best writing (speaking or reading) you have done in your composition class? Why?

In this chapter, I have drawn from the portfolio literature to discuss how socioliterate practices might be established in a variety of teaching environments. First, I talked about the general portfolio characteristics and discussed two models, one for reading and one for writing, that can be adapted to a wide variety of literacy contexts. Figure 3 illustrates the core entries in each of these models.

Then I discussed a specific experience with a linked-class portfolio model in my university. Working with the history professor was a positive learning experience for all involved. Not all of the linked classes on our campus are as well integrated, however. In most, the literacy and DS instructors meet occasionally to discuss students or content; very few integrate syllabi in this way, despite the fact that the arrangement is ideal. Whatever happens between the instructors, the linked classes have their

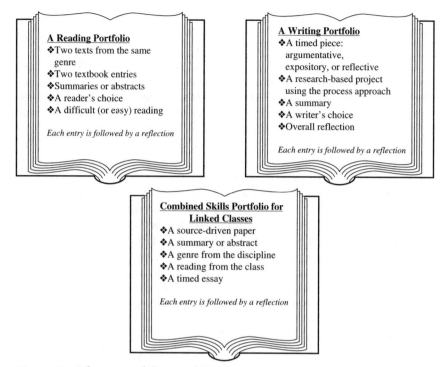

A Reading Portfolio
* ❖Two texts from the same genre
* ❖Two textbook entries
* ❖Summaries or abstracts
* ❖A reader's choice
* ❖A difficult (or easy) reading

Each entry is followed by a reflection

A Writing Portfolio
* ❖A timed piece: argumentative, expository, or reflective
* ❖A research-based project using the process approach
* ❖A summary
* ❖A writer's choice
* ❖Overall reflection

Each entry is followed by a reflection

Combined Skills Portfolio for Linked Classes
* ❖A source-driven paper
* ❖A summary or abstract
* ❖A genre from the discipline
* ❖A reading from the class
* ❖A timed essay

Each entry is followed by a reflection

Figure 3   Three portfolio models: Core entries.

own curricula, and they exploit the DS classes for academic situatedness, for faculty insights, for values, for texts, and for intertextual possibilities. Through this interaction with the DS classes and the use of the literacy portfolio syllabus, students are able to expand their questions and research and to explore their theories of texts, roles, and contexts within specific academic situations. As they read and write in their literacy classes, they are encouraged to develop a metacognitive awareness of their task representations and their strategies, often influenced by their personal motivations, past schooling, and genre knowledge. Though little has been said in this chapter about the development of student metalinguistic awareness, this is also an integral part of our classroom discussions and activities. Of particular value are the discussions of the rhetorical effects of grammatical choices (see Kolln, 1991) and the purposes that sentence-level elements might serve within discourses for the writers and their communities. Students work with grammar, mechanics, and vocabulary within texts selected from academic (and external) contexts. They talk about the importance of editing, particularly for certain audiences. They also consider how they can write to be heard (or read), to make their own argumentation distinct within the cacophony of disciplinary discourses. Understanding the social forces that drive texts is enabling, as our students have told us many times.

In the literacy classes using all three portfolio designs, the students consider various named texts as possible genre exemplars, hypothesizing about the kinds of shared knowledge that expert readers and writers must have. They discuss how they read different kinds of texts, and why and how they write different kinds of texts as well. They talk about their past text experiences and their current experiences with texts and tasks, developing an ever-widening theory of genre and strategies for processing discourses. They are encouraged not only to search out and exploit experts and sources of various kinds, but to discuss and critique, through their reflections, their successes and problems in approaching different tasks and the values that are found in the academic community.

Portfolios play an important part in managing the goals of a socioliterate program. These management tools require considerable cooperation and planning among faculty; however, we find that the work is well worth the effort, as we observe how students move in their reflections from their text autonomous theories to questions about the social forces influencing texts, about their own text histories, and about how their strategies must vary to meet many different kinds of rhetorical situations. Of course, literacy faculty can also benefit from portfolios; they make very interesting reading and contribute to joint curricular planning.

9 Conclusion

In an important article entitled "University in the Digital Age," Brown and Duguid (1995) ask why students and their parents sacrifice so much time, money, and energy for a postsecondary education, why this experience is so important to so many people throughout the world.[1] For students who plan to be an full-time academics, to teach in universities or conduct research, the answer may be fairly straightforward: "Universities provide access to communities of scholars and testimony for a student's experience among these communities" (1995, p. 4). However, many of the students enrolled in our literacy classes and our universities do not aspire to be fully initiated members of disciplinary communities or to devote their lives to academic study. Instead, they have chosen to go into business, computer technology, engineering, and other professions. For them, or perhaps for all students, the answer to this question is complex and revealing.

Parents and students often say that a university education is a "downpayment on a career" (Brown & Duguid, 1995, p. 6). They tell us that their degrees are "professional union cards," or that they have been assured by their secondary school teachers and counselors that with advanced degrees, they will be able to make "at least twice the salary of the average secondary school graduate." Others, including some university faculty, view education as a kind of "knowledge delivery service" (Brown & Duguid, 1995, p. 7). During postsecondary education, these people claim, knowledge is "deposited" into students, who are considered to be naive, empty vessels. In his famous *Pedagogy of the Oppressed*, Paulo Freire (1993, p. 53) describes this view:

Education thus becomes an act of depositing, in which the students are the depositories and the teacher is the depositor. Instead of communicating, the teacher issues communiqués and makes deposits which the students patiently receive, memorize, and repeat. This is the "banking" concept of education, in

1 Postsecondary education is referred to, quite logically, as tertiary education in many parts of the world.

151

which the scope of action allowed to the students extends only as far as receiving, filing and storing the deposits.[2]

However, postsecondary education should be, and often is, much more than a knowledge bank, for "the core of competency of universities is not transferring knowledge, but developing it, and that's done within intricate and robust networks and communities" (Brown & Duguid, 1995, p. 9). Using Toulmin (1972) and Lave and Wenger (1991) to support their argument, Brown and Duguid contend that a university education provides for student exposure to a variety of communities of practice in which they "get to know not just what the standard answers are, but the real questions and why they matter" (1995. p. 10).

These communities, "humanistic, natural scientific, social scientific alike, that make up the scattered discourse of modern scholarship are more than just intellectual coigns of vantage but are ways of being in the world" (Geertz, 1983, p. 155). Of what do these "ways of being" consist? Practitioners in English for Specific Purposes, noting that "ways of being" and literacy are inexorably linked, mention special uses of lexis and grammar, conceptual taxonomies, and ways of selecting, organizing, and presenting data through established genres. Composition theorists talk about rhetorical choices in argumentation, style, and use of visual representations. Gross (1991, p. 933), for example, argues that

. . . science is deeply rhetorical; stylistic choices conspire in the creation of the world as meant by science; organizational choices imitate the approved means of achieving access to the world.

The importance of a university education, then, lies in the realization that communities of practice are deeply value-laden and rhetorical: language, genres, methodologies, and the conventions that support them are what distinguish communities from each other, and, at times, bring them into conflict.

These claims are wonderful to contemplate, but they raise problems when applied to real academic literacy situations, several of which have been mentioned in this volume. One problem is that discipline-specific faculty may be unable or unwilling to reveal to students the conflicting and messy practices and varied languages and genres of their disciplines. Instead, they may assign textbooks that present consensual knowledge and "facts" in a digested form, and they may require writing assignments that are pedagogical rather than community-specific, even at advanced educational levels (see Kuhn, 1970; Myers, 1992). Chiseri-Strater (1991, p. 40) makes these comments about this apparent faculty reluctance:

2 Note that the drill and practice elements of the Traditional approaches, as well as the Behaviorist acquisition theories that supported them, are, in fact, banking approaches (see Richards & Rogers, 1986).

Nondisclosure about how scholars acquire their knowledge inadvertently misrepresents the nature of collaboration and interaction in higher education. Lack of modeling robs students of insights about the incubation process and denies them access to the messy rough-draft thinking involved in making meaning – from ideas, from texts, from colleagues.

Another problem that seems to be pervasive throughout the world relates to the naive view of literacy and critical thinking that appears to be held by the general public as well as by many faculty and administrators (see McKay, 1993). Because many believe that even second or foreign language literacy acquisition is simple, consisting of basic skills that can be "fixed" by practitioners in a short period of time, faculty and administrators often fail to understand their responsibilities in promoting literacy in every class through the active teaching of reading and writing as related to "ways of being" in the disciplines. Thus, the entire responsibility for student literacy, and its intricate relationship with communities of practice and their genres, falls, in many cases, on marginalized literacy units within an academic context.

Respected literacy practitioners argue that because of the complicated nature of disciplinary practices, the reluctance of DS faculty, and, not incidentally, the situated variations within each classroom, we cannot possibly prepare students for the many texts, roles, and contexts to which they will be exposed within the university and beyond. In an important article entitled "Initiating ESL Students into the Academic Discourse Community: How Far Should We Go?," Spack tells us that we should leave the initiation into disciplinary communities to the initiated, and that "the English composition course . . . should be a humanities course: a place where students are provided the enrichment of reading and writing that provokes thought and fosters their intellectual and ethical development" (1988, p. 46). She goes on to say that

. . . we do not have to change our orientation completely, assign tasks we ourselves cannot master, or limit our assignments to prescribed, rule-governed tasks. We can instead draw on our own knowledge and abilities as we strengthen and expand the knowledge and abilities of our students (p. 47).

After completing extensive, situated research, Prior (1995, p. 76) argues, quite convincingly, that we could not possibly help students to complete tasks in all academic environments, since "tasks are fundamentally situated and multiple" (see also Nelson, 1990). Prior also maintains that for the same reasons, we must be very careful about a formulaic teaching of genres. He says:

Genres may represent relatively stable configurations in the ways texts are produced and received, but genres are also dynamic – multivoiced, multigoaled phenomena generated by the complexly orchestrated interaction of centripetal and centrifugal forces in the unfolding of micro- and macro-histories of the world. Genres in this view emerge as considerably more complex than typical notions of genre, but this specification also offers a principled way to explore how genres are employed, reconfigured, and reaccentuated as situations vary (p. 58).

What, then, do we do? Do we retreat to our classrooms to teach only what we already know or to orient students to our particular interests, ideologies, and values? Do we return to the Traditional teaching of grammar and paragraph structures? Do we teach humanities and ethics? Do we wring our hands and bemoan our marginality? I think not. Instead, we should capitalize upon our unique abilities to explore academic worlds: their languages, their genres, their values, and their literacies, remembering at all times that these worlds are complex and evolving, conflicted and messy. Only through being involved in research, teaching, and learning across the disciplines, and encouraging our students to do the same, can we hope to give to our classes the opportunities to explore, investigate, and critique their current and future communities of practice.

In this volume I have suggested some ways in which we can fully live out our unique roles within academic contexts. Chapters 1, 2, and 3 laid the groundwork, for I believe that we must come to terms with our own theories, and those of others, before we can make intelligent pedagogical and investigative choices. In Chapters 5 and 6 I suggested how we, and our students, can be involved in ongoing research into the texts, roles, and contexts of our academic communities. In Chapters 7 and 8 I outlined some basic curricular tenets for our classes, and I proposed class goals for literacy students. I then provided three examples of portfolio-based curricula in which most, if not all, of these goals can be met.

It is unfortunate that the most important work of a university, the advancement of literacies within communities of practice, is often marginalized. Rather than contributing to this marginalization, we can – and should – promote a more sophisticated understanding of literacies on our campuses, and, while doing so, motivate our students to undertake difficult academic work.

References

Adams, T. W. (1989). *Inside textbooks: What students need to know*. Reading, MA: Addison-Wesley.

Alred, G. A., & Thelen, E. A. (1993). Are textbooks contributions to scholarship? *College Composition and Communication, 44,* 446–477.

Arden-Close, C. (1993). Language problems in science lectures to non-native speakers. *English for Specific Purposes, 12,* 251–261.

Armbruster, B., & Anderson, T. (1984). *Producing "considerate" expository text: Or easy reading is damned hard writing*. (Reading Education Rep. No. 46). Urbana-Champaign, IL: University of Illinois, Center for the Study of Reading.

Arnold, E. (1991). Authenticity revisited: How real is real? *English for Specific Purposes, 10,* 237–244.

Aronowitz, S., & Giroux, H. A. (1991). *Education under siege*. South Hadley, MA: Bergin.

Arrington, P., & Rose, S. K. (1987). Prologues to what is possible: Introductions as metadiscourse. *College Composition and Communication, 38,* 306–318.

Bakhtin, M. M. (1981). *The dialogic imagination: Four essays by M. M. Bakhtin*. (C. Emerson & M. Holquist, Trans.). M. Holquist (Ed.). Austin: University of Texas Press.

Bakhtin, M. M. (1986). *Speech genres and other late essays*. (V. W. Mc Gee, Trans.). C. Emerson & M. Holquist (Eds.). Austin: University of Texas Press.

Barbara, L., Celani, M. A. A., Collins, H., & Scott, M. (1996). A survey of communication patterns in the Brazilian business context. *English for Specific Purposes, 15,* 57–72.

Barnett, M. (1989). *More than meets the eye: Foreign language learner reading, theory and practice*. Englewood Cliffs, NJ: Prentice Hall Regents.

Bartholomae, D. (1985). Inventing the university. In M. Rose (Ed.), *When a writer can't write: Studies in writer's block and other composing process problems* (pp. 134–165). New York: Guilford Press.

Bazerman, C. (1994). Where is the classroom? In A. Freedman & P. Medway (Eds.), *Learning and teaching genre* (pp. 25–30). Portsmouth, NH: Heinemann/Boynton-Cook.

Belanoff, P., & Dickson, M. (Eds.). (1991). *Portfolios: Process and product*. Portsmouth, NH: Heinemann/Boynton-Cook.

Belcher, D., & Braine, G. (Eds.). (1995). *Academic writing in a second language: Essays on research and pedagogy*. Norwood, NJ: Ablex.

Benesch, S. (1988). *Ending remediation: Linking ESL and content in higher education.* Washington, DC: TESOL.

Benesch, S. (1996, March). *Critical interventions with university faculty.* Paper presented at the 30th Annual TESOL Convention, Chicago, IL.

Benson, K. (1996). *How do students and faculty perceive graduate writing tasks? A case study of a Japanese student in a graduate program in linguistics.* Unpublished manuscript, San Diego State University.

Bereiter, C., & Scardamalia, M. (1989). Intentional learning as a goal of instruction. In J. Resnick (Ed.), *Knowing, learning* (pp. 361–392). Hillsdale, NJ: Lawrence Erlbaum.

Berkenkotter, C., & Huckin, T. (1995). *Genre knowledge in disciplinary communities.* Hillsdale, NJ: Lawrence Erlbaum.

Berlin, J. (1988). Rhetoric and ideology in the writing class. *College English, 50,* 477–494.

Bernhart, E. B. (1991). *Reading development in a second language: Theoretical, empirical & classroom perspectives.* Norwood, NJ: Ablex.

Bhatia, V. J. (1993). *Analyzing genre: Language use in professional settings.* London & New York: Longman.

Biber, D., Conrad, S., Helt, M. E., Burgess, J. A., & Reppen, R. (1996, March). *Corpus-based perspectives on discourse.* A colloquium presented at the Annual Convention of the American Association of Applied Lingusitics, Chicago, IL.

Bintz, W. P., & Harste, J. (1991). A vision for the future of assessment in whole language classrooms. In B. Harp (Ed.), *Assessment and evaluation in whole language classrooms* (pp. 219–242). Norwood, MA: Christopher Gordon.

Black, L., Daiker, D. A., Sommers, J., & Stygall, G. (1994). *New directions in portfolio assessment: Reflective practice, critical theory, and large-scale scoring.* Portsmouth, NH: Boynton-Cook.

Briggs, C., & Baumann, R. (1992). Genre, intertextuality, and social power. *Journal of Linguistic Anthropology, 2,* 131–172.

Brill, D. (1994, November). What's free of fat and cholesterol, costs 4 cents per serving, and has more carbo than pasta? Rice! *Bicycling,* 86–87.

Brinton, D. M., Snow, M. A., & Wesche, M. B. (1989). *Content-based second language instruction.* New York: Newbury House.

Brosnahan, I., Coe, R., & Johns, A. M. (1987). Discourse analysis of written texts in an overseas teacher training program. *English Quarterly (Canada), 7,* 16–25.

Brown, J. S., Collins, A., & Duguid, P. (1989). Situated cognition and the culture of learning. *Educational Researcher, 18,* 32–42.

Brown, J. S., & Duguid, P. (1995, July 26). Universities in the digital age. *Xerox Palo Alto Paper.* Palo Alto, CA: Xerox Corporation.

Calfee, R. (1994). Critical literacy: Reading and writing for a new millennium. In N. J. Ellsworth, C. N. Hedley, & A. N. Baratta (Eds.), *Literacy: A redefinition* (pp. 19–38). Hillsdale, NJ: Lawrence Erlbaum.

Carrell, P. L., Pharis, B. G., & Liberto, J. C. (1989). Metacognitive strategy training for ESL reading. *TESOL Quarterly, 23(4),* 647–678.

Carson, J. G. (1993, April). *Academic literacy demands of the undergraduate curriculum: Literacy activities integrating skills.* Paper presented at the International TESOL Conference, Atlanta, GA.

Carson, J. G., Chase, N., Gibson, S., & Hargrove, M. (1992). Literacy demands of the undergraduate curriculum. *Reading Research and Instruction, 31,* 25–50.

Casanave, C. P. (1992). Cultural diversity and socialization: A case study of a Hispanic woman in a doctoral program in Sociology. In D. Murray (Ed.), *Diversity as a resource: Redefining cultural literacy* (pp. 148–182). Arlington, VA: TESOL.

Chapman, M. (1994). The emergence of genres: Some findings from the examination of first-grade writing. *Written Communication, 11,* 348–380.

Chiseri-Strater, E. (1991). *Academic literacies: The public and private discourse of university students.* Portsmouth, NH: Heinemann/Boynton-Cook.

Christie, F. (1993). The "received tradition" of literacy teaching: The decline of rhetoric and corruption of grammar. In B. Green (Ed.), *The insistence of the letter: Literacy studies and curriculum theorizing* (pp. 75–106). London: Falmer Press/University of Pittsburgh Press.

Clifford, J. (1986). Introduction: Partial truths. In J. Clifford & G. Marcus (Eds.), *Writing culture: The poetics and politics of ethnography* (pp. 1–26). Berkeley & Los Angeles: University of California Press.

Coe, R. M. (1987). An apology for form; or, who took the form out of the process? *College English, 49,* 13–28.

Coe, R. M. (1993, March/April). *Prophesying after the event: The archeology and ecology of genre.* Paper presented at the Conference on College Composition and Communication, San Diego, CA.

Coe, R. M. (1994). Teaching genre as process. In A. Freedman & P. Medway (Eds.), *Learning and teaching genre* (pp. 157–69). Portsmouth, NH: Heinemann/Boynton-Cook.

Connor, U. (1987). Argumentative patterns in student essays: Cross-cultural differences. In U. Connor & R. B. Kaplan (Eds.), *Writing across languages: Analysis of L2 text* (pp. 57–71). Reading, MA: Addison-Wesley.

Connor, U. (1996). *Contrastive rhetoric: Cross-cultural aspects of second language writing.* New York: Cambridge University Press.

Connor, U., and Johns, A. (Eds.). (1990). *Coherence in writing: Research and pedagogical perspectives.* Alexandria, VA: Teachers of English to Speakers of Other Languages.

Cook-Gumperz, J. (Ed.). (1986). *The social construction of literacy.* Cambridge: Cambridge University Press.

Cope, B., & Kalantzis, M. (1993). Introduction: How a genre approach to literacy can transform the way writing is taught. In B. Cope & M. Kalantzis (Eds.), *The powers of literacy* (pp. 1–21). London: Falmer Press.

Crismore, A. (1985). *The case for a rhetorical perspective on learning from texts: Exploring metadiscourse.* (Tech. Rep. No. 342). Urbana-Champaign, IL: University of Illinois, Center for the Study of Reading.

Davies, F. (1995). *Introducing reading.* London: Penguin.

DeCarrico, J., & Nattinger, J. R. (1988). Lexical phrases for the comprehension of academic lectures. *English for Specific Purposes, 7,* 91–102.

Derewianka, B. (1990). *Exploring how texts work.* Maryborough, Victoria: Australian Primary English Teaching Association.

Dewey, J. (1916). *Democracy in education: An introduction to the philosophy of education.* New York: Macmillan.

DiPardo, A. (1993). *A kind of passport: A basic writing adjunct program and the challenge of student diversity.* Urbana, IL: National Council of Teachers of English.

Doheny-Farina, S., & Odell, L. (1985). Ethnographic research on writing: Assumptions and methodology. In L. Odell & D. Gaswami (Eds.), *Writing in nonacademic settings* (pp. 503–535). New York: Guilford Press.

Dudley-Evans, T. (1995). Common-core and specific approaches to teaching academic writing. In D. Belcher & G. Braine (Eds.), *Academic writing in a second language: Essays on research and pedagogy* (pp. 293–312). Norwood, NJ: Ablex.

Edelsky, C., Altwerger, B., & Flores, B. (1991). *Whole Language: What's the difference?* Portsmouth, NH: Heinemann/Boynton-Cook.

Elbow, P. (1981). *Embracing contraries: Explorations in learning and teaching.* New York: Oxford University Press.

Elbow, P. (1991). Reflections on academic discourse. *College English, 53(2),* 135–155.

Enkvist, N. E. (1990). Seven problems in the study of coherence and interpretability. In U. Connor & A. M. Johns (Eds.), *Coherence in writing: Research and pedagogical perspectives* (pp. 9–28). Alexandria, VA: TESOL.

Eskey, D. E. (1992). Syllabus design in content-based instruction. *The CATESOL Journal, 5,* 11–24.

Fahenstock, J. (1986). Accommodating science. *Written Communication, 3,* 275–296.

Fairclough, N. (1992). *Discourse and social change.* Cambridge, UK: Polity Press.

Feathers, K. M. (1993). *Infotext: Reading and learning.* Markham, Ont: Pippin.

Fielden, C. (1995, May). *Obligatory components of obituaries across discourse communities and cultures.* Paper presented in the Linguistics Seminar, San Diego State University, San Diego, CA.

Finegan, E. (1996, March). *The expression of epistemic stance in three registers of English: Conversation, news writing and academic prose.* Paper presented at the Annual Conference of the American Association of Applied Linguistics, Chicago, IL.

Fish, S. (1985). Consequences. *Critical Inquiry, 11,* 433–458.

Fitzgerald, K. R. (1988). Rhetorical implications of school discourse for writing placement. *Journal of Basic Writing, 7(1),* 61–72.

Flowerdew, J. (Ed.). (1995). *Academic Listening.* New York: Cambridge University Press.

Francis, G. (1994). Grammar teaching in schools: What should teachers be aware of? *Language Awareness, 3,* 221–236.

Frazier, D. M., & Paulson, F. L. (1992, February). How portfolios motivate reluctant writers. *Educational Leadership,* 62–65.

Freedman, A., & Medway, P. (Eds.). (1994a). *Learning and teaching genre.* Portsmouth, NH: Heinemann/Boynton-Cook.

Freedman, A., & Medway, P. (1994b). Introduction. In A. Freedman & P. Medway (Eds.), *Learning and teaching genre* (pp. 1–22). Portsmouth, NH: Heinemann/Boynton-Cook.

Freire, P. (1993). *Pedagogy of the oppressed.* New York: Continuum Press.

Fulweiler, T. (1982). The personal connection: Journal writing across the curriculum. In T. Fulweiler & A. Young (Eds.), *Language connections: Writing and reading across the curriculum* (pp. 15–32). Urbana, IL: National Council of Teachers of English.

Gee, J. (1991). Socio-cultural approaches to literacy. *Annual Review of Applied Linguistics, 12,* 31–48.

Gee, Y. (1992). How can ESL and content teachers work effectively together in adjunct courses? *CATESOL Journal, 5,* 85–92.

Geertz, C. (1983). *Local knowledge: Further essays in interpretive anthropology.* New York: Basic Books.

Geertz, C. (1988). *Words and lives: The anthropologist as author.* Palo Alto, CA: Stanford University Press.

Geisler, C. (1991). Toward a socio-cognitive model of literacy: Constructing mental models in a philosophical conversation. In C. Bazerman & J. Paradis (Eds.), *Textual dynamics and the professions* (pp. 171–190). Madison: University of Wisconsin Press.

Geisler, C. (1994). Literacy and expertise in the academy. *Language and Learning Across the Disciplines, 1,* 35–57.

Gernsbacher, M. A. (1990). *Language comprehension as structure building.* Hillsdale, NJ: Lawrence Erlbaum.

Giltrow, G., & Valiquette, M. (1994). Genre and knowledge: Students' writing in the disciplines. In A. Freedman & P. Medway (Eds.), *Learning and teaching genre* (pp. 47–62). Portsmouth, NH: Heinemann/Boynton-Cook.

Giroux, H. A. (1983). *Theory and resistance in education.* South Hadley, MA: Bergin.

Gordon, C. M., & Hanauer, D. (1995). The interaction between task and meaning construction in EFL reading comprehension tests. *TESOL Quarterly, 29,* 299–324.

Gould, S. J. (1985). *The flamingo's smile.* New York: Norton.

Grabe, W. (1988). Reassessing the term "interactive." In P. Carrell, J. Devine, & D. Eskey (Eds.), *Interactive approaches to second language reading* (pp. 56–72). New York: Cambridge University Press.

Gross, A. G. (1991). Does the rhetoric of science matter? The case of the floppy-eared rabbits. *College English, 53,* 933–943.

Haas, C. (1994). Learning to read biology: One student's rhetorical development in college. *Written Communication, 11,* 43–84.

Halliday, M. A. K. (1978). *Language as a social semiotic: The social interpretation of language and meaning.* London: Edward Arnold.

Halliday, M. A. K. (1991, March/April). The notion of "context" in language education. In T. Le & M. Mc Causland (Eds.), *Language education: International development* (pp. 4–26). Proceedings of the International Conference, Ho Chi Minh City, Vietnam.

Halliday, M. A. K. (1993). Some grammatical problems in scientific English. In M. A. K. Halliday & J. R. Martin (Eds.), *Writing science: Literacy and discursive power* (pp. 69–85). Pittsburgh, PA: University of Pittsburgh Press.

Halliday, M. A. K., & Hasan, R. (1976). *Cohesion in English.* London: Longman.

Halliday, M. A. K., & Martin, J. R. (1993). *Writing science: Literacy and discursive power.* Pittsburgh, PA: University of Pittsburgh Press.

Halliday, M. A. K., McIntosh, A., & Strevens, P. (1964). *The linguistic sciences and language teaching.* Bloomington: Indiana University Press.

Harris, C. B. (1990). Report from the Eastern shore: The English coalition conference. In G. E. Hawisher & A. O. Soter (Eds.), *On literacy and its teaching: Issues in English education* (pp. 19–35). Albany: State University of New York Press.

Harste, J. (1990, January). Point/counterpoint: State-by-state comparison on national assessments. *Reading Today, 7,* 12–13.

Heald-Taylor, G. (1991). *Whole Language strategies for ESL students.* San Diego, CA: Dominie Press.

Heath, S. B. (1986). Sociocultural contexts of language development. In *Beyond language: Social and cultural factors in schooling language minority students* (pp. 143–186). Developed by Bilingual Education Office, California State Department of Education. Los Angeles, CA: Evaluation, Dissemination, and Assessment Center, California State University.

Herndl, C. G. (1993). Reaching discourse and reproducing culture: A critique of research and pedagogy in professional and non-academic writing. *College Composition and Communication, 43,* 214–224.

Herrington, A., & Moran, C. (1992). Writing in the disciplines: A prospect. In A. Herrington and C. Moran (Eds.), *Writing, teaching and learning in the disciplines* (pp. 231–244). New York: Modern Language Association.

Hinds, J. (1987). Reader versus writer responsibility: A new typology. In U. Connor & R. B. Kaplan (Eds.), *Writing across languages: An analysis of L2 texts* (pp. 141–152). Reading, MA: Addison-Wesley.

Hohl, M. (1982, Summer). Necessary English at UPM: A faculty survey. *Team, 42,* 15–40. Dhahran, Saudi Arabia: University of Petroleum & Minerals.

Horowitz, D. M. (1986a). What professors actually require: Academic tasks for the ESL classroom. *TESOL Quarterly, 20,* 445–462.

Horowitz, D. M. (1986b). Essay examination prompts and the teaching of academic writing. *English for Specific Purposes, 5,* 107–120.

Huckin, T. (1987, March). *Surprise value in scientific discourse.* Paper presented at the Conference on College Composition and Communication, Atlanta, GA.

Ibrahim, A. H. (1993). Ethnography in ESP: The quest for description. *ESP Malaysia, 1,* 102–117.

January, A. J. (1995). *The court report as genre.* Unpublished manuscript, San Diego State University.

Johns, A. M. (1981a). Cohesion in written business discourse: Some contrasts. *English for Specific Purposes, 1,* 35–44.

Johns, A. M. (1981b). Necessary English: A faculty survey. *TESOL Quarterly, 15,* 51–58.

Johns, A. M. (1985). The new authenticity and the preparation of commercial reading texts for lower-level ESP students. *CATESOL Occasional Papers, 11,* 103–107.

Johns, A. M. (1986). *Writing tasks and evaluation in lower-division classes: A comparison of two- and four-year postsecondary institutions.* ERIC: Clearinghouse on Languages and Linguistics, Washington, DC: Center for Applied Linguistics.

Johns, A. M. (1990a). L1 composition theories: Implications for developing theories of L2 composition. In B. Kroll (Ed.), *Second language writing: Research insights for the classroom* (pp. 24–36). Cambridge: Cambridge University Press.

Johns, A. M. (1990b). Coherence as a cultural phenomenon: Employing ethnographic principles in the academic milieu. In U. Connor & A. M. Johns (Eds.), *Coherence in writing: Research and pedagogical perspectives* (pp. 209–226). Alexandria, VA: TESOL.

Johns, A. M. (1991). Faculty assessment of ESL student literacy skills: Implications for writing assessment. In L. Hamp-Lyons (Ed.), *Assessing second language writing in academic contexts* (pp. 167–179). Norwood, NJ: Ablex.

Johns, A. M. (1992). Toward developing a cultural repertoire: A case study of Lao freshmen. In D. Murray (Ed.), *Diversity as a resource: Redefining cultural literacy* (pp. 183–201). Arlington, VA: TESOL.

Johns, A. M. (1993). Written argumentation for real audiences: Suggestions for teacher research and classroom practices. *TESOL Quarterly, 27(1)*, 74–90.

Johns, T. F., & Davies, F. (1983). Text as a vehicle for information: The classroom use of written texts in teaching reading in a foreign language. *Reading in a Foreign Language, 1,* 1–19.

Johns, T. F., & Dudley-Evans, A. (1980). An experiment in team-teaching of overseas postgraduate students of transportation and plant biology. *ELT Documents 106: Team Teaching in ESP.* London: The British Council (ETIC).

Johnson, D. M., & Roen, D. H. (Eds.). (1989). *Richness in writing: Empowering ESL students.* New York: Longman.

Kay, H. (1993, April). *Genre: A view from the classroom.* Paper presented at the Regional English Language Centre Annual Conference, Singapore.

Kent, T. (1993). *Paralogic rhetoric: A theory of communicative interaction.* London: Associated University Presses.

Khoo, R. (1993, April). *Empowering the EBT practitioner: A project perspective.* Plenary presented at the RELC Regional Seminar on Language for Specific Purposes: Problems & Prospects, Singapore.

Killingsworth, M. J. (1992). Discourse communities – local and global. *Rhetoric Review, 11,* 110–122.

Kiniry, M., & Rose, M. (1993). *Critical strategies for academic thinking and writing: A text and reader.* Boston: Bedford Books/St. Martin's Press.

Kishida, E. (1995). *The Japanese newspaper obituary: A highly conventionalized text.* Unpublished manuscript, San Diego State University.

Kolln, M. (1991). *Rhetorical grammar: Grammatical choices, rhetorical effects.* New York: Macmillan.

Kress, G. (1985). *Linguistic processes in socio-cultural practice.* New York: Oxford University Press.

Kuhn, T. S. (1963). The function of dogma in scientific research. In A. C. Crombie (Ed.), *Scientific Change* (pp. 347–369). London: Heinemann.

Kuhn, T. S. (1970). *The structure of scientific revolutions* (2nd ed.). Chicago, IL: University of Chicago Press.

Kumaravadivelu, B. (1994). The postmethod condition: (E)merging strategies for second/foreign language teaching. *TESOL Quarterly, 28,* 27–48.

Larson, R. L. (1982). The "research paper" in the writing course: A non-form of writing. *College English, 44,* 811–816.

Latour, B., & Woolgar, S. (1986). *Laboratory life: The social construction of scientific facts.* (2nd ed.). Princeton, NJ: Princeton University Press.

Lautamatti, L. (1987). Observations on the development of the topic in simplified discourse. In U. Connor & R. B. Kaplan (Eds.), *Writing across languages: Analysis of L2 texts* (pp. 92–126). Reading, MA: Addison-Wesley.

Lave, J., & Wenger, E. (1991). *Situated learning: Legitimate peripheral participation*. New York: Cambridge University Press.

Lebauer, R. (1984). Using lecture transcripts in EAP lecture comprehension courses. *TESOL Quarterly, 8*, 41–54.

Leki, I. (1992). *Understanding ESL writers*. Portsmouth, NH: Heinemann/Boynton-Cook.

Leki, I. (1995). Coping strategies of ESL students in writing tasks across the curriculum. *TESOL Quarterly, 29*, 235–260.

MacDonald, S. P. (1990). The literary argument and its discursive conventions. In W. Nash (Ed.), *The writing scholar: Studies in academic discourse* (pp. 31–62). (Written Communication Annual, #3). Newbury Park, CA: Sage.

Markee, N. (1986). The relevance of socio-political factors in communicative course design. *English for Specific Purposes, 5*, 3–16.

Martin, J. (1985). *Factual writing: Exploring and challenging social reality*. Oxford: Oxford University Press.

Martin, N. (1992). Language across the curriculum: Where it began and what it promises. In A. Herrington & C. Moran (Eds.), *Writing, teaching and learning in the disciplines* (pp. 231–244). New York: Modern Language Association.

Mauranen, A. (1993). Contrastive ESP rhetoric: Metatext in Finnish-English economic texts. *English for Specific Purposes, 12*, 3–22.

McCarthy, L. P. (1987). A stranger in a strange land: A college student writing across the curriculum. *Research in the Teaching of English, 21*, 223–265.

McKay, S. L. (1993). *Agendas for second language literacy*. New York: Cambridge University Press.

McKenna, E. (1987). Preparing foreign students to enter discourse communities in the United States. *English for Specific Purposes, 6*, 187–202.

Miller, C. (1984). Genre as social action. *Quarterly Journal of Speech, 70*, 151–167.

Mohan, B. B. (1986). *Language and content*. Reading, MA: Addison-Wesley.

Montford, A. (1975). Principles and procedures for text simplification in the teaching of English for Science and Technology. *Edutech:* Naucalpan, Mexico: Universidad Autonoma and Metropolitana (Qulio), 36–43.

Muchiri, M. N., Mulamba, N. G., Myers, G., & Ndoloi, D. B. (1995). Importing composition: Teaching and researching academic writing beyond North America. *College Composition and Communication, 46*, 175–198.

Myers, G. (1989). The pragmatics of politeness in scientific knowledge. *Applied Linguistics, 10*, 1–35.

Myers, G. (1992). Textbooks and the sociology of scientific knowledge. *English for Specific Purposes, 11*, 3–18.

Nation, I. S. P. (1990). *Teaching and learning vocabulary*. New York: Newbury House.

Neilsen, L. (1989). *Literacy and living: The literate lives of three adults*. Portsmouth, NH: Heinemann/Boynton-Cook.

Nelson, J. (1990). This was an easy assignment: Examining how students interpret academic writing tasks. *Research in the Teaching of English, 24*, 262–296.

Olsen, L. A., & Huckin, T. N. (1990). Point-driven understanding in engineering lecture comprehension. *English for Specific Purposes, 9,* 33–48.

Pang, S. G. S., & Heng, C. S. (1993). The use of English in the commercial sector of the Malaysian economy: Perspectives from potential employers and employees. *ESP Malaysia: A National Journal on English for Specific Purposes, 1,* 128–147.

Pena, A. (1995). *Obituaries as genre: A study from Brazilian newspapers.* Unpublished manuscript, San Diego State University.

Peyton, J. K. (1987). *Dialogue journal writing with limited-English-proficiency students.* Washington, DC: ERIC Clearinghouse on Languages and Linguistics. (ERIC Document Reproduction Service, #287–308).

Praninskas, J. (1972). *American university word list.* London: Longman.

Prior, P. (1991). Contextualizing writing and response in a graduate seminar. *Written Communication, 8,* 267–310.

Prior, P. (1994). Response, revision and disciplinarity: A microhistory of a dissertation prospectus in sociology. *Written Communication, 11,* 483–533.

Prior, P. (1995). Redefining the task: An ethnographic examination of writing and response in graduate seminars. In D. Belcher & G. Braine (Eds.), *Academic writing in a second language: Essays on research & pedagogy* (pp. 47–82). Norwood, NJ: Ablex.

Purves, A. C. (1990). *The scribal society: An essay on literacy and schooling in the information age.* New York: Longman.

Purves, A. C. (1991). The textual contract: Literacy as common knowledge and conventional wisdom. In E. M. Jennings & A. C. Purves (Eds.), *Literate systems and individual lives: Perspectives on literacy and schooling* (pp. 51–72). Albany: State University of New York.

Purves, A. C., Quattrini, J. A., & Sullivan, C. I. (1995). *Creating the writing portfolio.* Lincolnwood, IL: NTC Publishing.

Rafoth, B. A. (1990). The concept of discourse community: Descriptive and explanatory adequacy. In G. Kirsch & D. H. Roen (Eds), *A sense of audience in written communication* (pp. 140–152). *Written Communication Annual, Vol. 5.* Newbury Park, CA: Sage.

Raimes, A. (1990). The TOEFL Test of Written English: Some causes for concern. *TESOL Quarterly, 24,* 427–442.

Raimes, A. (1991). Instructional balance: From theories to practices in the teaching of writing. In J. Alatis (Ed.), *Linguistics and language pedagogy.* Georgetown University Roundtable on Languages and Linguistics (pp. 238–249). Washington, DC: Georgetown University Press.

Ramanathan, V., & Kaplan, R. B. (1996). Audience and voice in current L1 composition textbooks: Some implications for L2 student writers. *Journal of Second Language Writing, 5,* 21–33.

Ratterey, O. M. T. (1985). Expanding roles for summarized information. *Written Communication, 2,* 257–272.

Richards, J. C., & Rodgers, T. S. (1986). *Approaches and methods in language teaching.* Cambridge: Cambridge University Press.

Richardson, P. W. (1994). Language as personal resource and as social construction: Competing views of literacy in pedagogy in Australia. In A. Freedman & P. Medway (Eds.), *Learning and teaching genre* (pp. 117–142). Portsmouth, NH: Heinemann/Boynton-Cook.

Rigg, P. (1991). Whole Language in TESOL. *TESOL Quarterly, 25,* 521–542.

Robinson, J. L. (1983). The social context of literacy. In P. L. Stock (Ed.), *Forum: Essays on theory and practice in the teaching of writing* (pp. 243–253). Portsmouth, NH: Heinemann/Boynton-Cook.

Rodriguez, R. (1982). *Hunger of memory: The education of Richard Rodriguez.* New York: Bantam Books.

Rose, M. (1989). *Lives on the boundary: The struggles and achievements of America's underprepared.* New York: Free Press.

Rosen, N. G. (1992). How are content-based instructional practices reflected in sheltered English? *CATESOL Journal, 5,* 109–112.

Russell, D. R. (1991). *Writing in the academic disciplines, 1870–1990: A curricular history.* Carbondale, IL: Southern Illinois University Press.

Sapir, E. (1909). *Wishram Texts.* Publications of the American Ethnological Society (#2). Leiden: E. J. Brill.

Schneider, M., & Fujishima, N. K. (1995). When practice doesn't make perfect: The case of a graduate ESL student. In D. Belcher & G. Braine (Eds.), *Academic writing in a second language: Essays on research & pedagogy* (pp. 3–22). Norwood, NJ: Ablex.

Silva, T. (1990). Second language composition instruction: Developments, issues and directions in ESL. In B. Kroll (Ed.), *Second language writing: Research insights for the classroom* (pp. 11–23). Cambridge: Cambridge University Press.

Skinner, B. F. (1957). *Verbal behavior.* New York: Appleton-Century-Crofts.

Spack, R. (1988). Initiating ESL students into the academic discourse community: How far should we go? *TESOL Quarterly, 22,* 29–52.

Spindler, G. (1982). Introduction. In G. Spindler (Ed.), *Doing the ethnography of schooling: Educational anthropology in action* (pp. 6–7). New York: Holt, Rinehart and Winston.

Stoller, F., & Grabe, W. (1995, March). *New directions in content-based instruction.* Presentation at the 29th Annual Convention of the Teachers of English to Speakers of Other Languages (TESOL), Long Beach, CA.

Swales, J. M. (1981). *Aspects of article introductions.* Birmingham, UK: The University of Aston Language Studies Unit.

Swales, J. M. (1988a). *Episodes in ESP: A source and reference book on the development of English for science and technology.* New York: Prentice Hall.

Swales, J. M. (1988b). Discourse communities, genres and English as an international language. *World Englishes, 7,* 211–220.

Swales, J. M. (1990). *Genre analysis: English in academic and research settings.* New York: Cambridge University Press.

Swales, J. M. (1993). Genre and engagement. *La revue belge de philologic et l'histoire.* (Fasc 3.: Langues et litteratures modernes, 71, pp. 687–698).

Swales, J. M. (1995). The role of the textbook in EAP writing research. *TESOL Quarterly, 14,* 3–18.

Swales, J. M., & Feak, C. B. (1994). *Academic writing for graduate students: Essential tasks and skills.* Ann Arbor: University of Michigan Press.

Tadros, A. A. (1989). Predictive categories in university textbooks. *English for Specific Purposes, 8,* 17–32.

Tannen, D. (1986). *That's not what I meant: How conversational style makes or breaks your relations with others.* New York: W. Morrow.

Tannen, D. (1994). *Talking from 9–5: How women's and men's conversational styles affect who gets heard, who gets credit, and what gets done at work.* New York: W. Morrow.

Tarone, E., Dwyer, S., Gillette, S., & Icke, V. (1981). On the use of the passive in two astrophysics journal papers. *English for Specific Purposes, 1,* 123–140.

Tierney, R. J. (1985). The reading-writing relationship: A glimpse of some facets. *Reading-Canada-Lecture, 3,* 109–116.

Tierney, R. J., Carter, M. A., & Desai, L. E. (1991). *Portfolio assessment in the reading-writing classroom.* Norwood, MA: Christopher-Gordon.

Toulmin, S. (1958). *The uses of argument.* Cambridge: Cambridge University Press.

Toulmin, S. (1972). *Human understanding: The collective use and evolution of concepts.* Princeton, NJ: Princeton University Press.

Walvoord, B. E., & McCarthy L. P. (1990). *Thinking and writing in college: A naturalistic study of students in four disciplines.* Champaign-Urbana, IL: National Council of Teachers of English.

Whorf, B. L. (1956). *Language thought and reality: Selected essays.* J. B. Carroll (Ed.), Cambridge, MA, & New York: M.I.T. Press & John Wiley.

Widdowson, H. G. (1993). The relevant conditions of language use and learning. In M. Krueger & F. Ryan (Eds.), *Language and content: Discipline-and content-based approaches to language study* (pp. 27–36). Lexington, MA: D. C. Heath.

Williams, J. (1989). *Style: Ten lessons in clarity and grace.* (3rd. ed.). Glenview, IL: Scott, Foresman.

Zamel, V. (1984). The author responds. *TESOL Quarterly, 18,* 154–157.

Zebroski, J. T. (1986, Winter). The uses of theory: A Vygotskian approach to composition. *The Writing Instructor, 5,* 57–67.

Index